An
Historical
Scrapbook

*containing more than fifty photographs and
illustrations*

A collection of pictorial essays of the life and times of
people, places and events in the Chesterfield area

By *David Jenkins*

Foreword

Field Marshall Viscount Lord Wavell, in his introduction to Other Men's Flowers, *a collection of his favourite poetry, likens one section of the selection to the contents of the brocade rag bag that his mother carried around all the stations his father was posted to. My essays, loosely related to Derbyshire and particularly Chesterfield, are similarly a rag bag of local history. By kind permission of the Editor, they are reprinted from* Reflections Magazine, *where they first appeared*

David E. Jenkins

Chesterfield

ISBN: 978-0-9525678-5-1

Published 2008 by Bannister Publications, 118 Saltergate, Chesterfield S40 1NG. Printed by the MPG Books Group in the UK © *David Edward Jenkins, 2009*

For my wife, Elaine,

ever a patient stalwart

Contents

A view of Chesterfield

ON A SUMMER'S DAY IN 1812, the year after Jane Austen published *Sense and Sensibility*, a little known water colourist, Mr. Pickering, set up his easel on Boythorpe hill and turned out a picture of pre-industrial Chesterfield set in a romanticised rural setting. The painting today hangs, surprisingly, not in the Borough's art gallery, but in a back room in the library.

In the foreground Pickering depicts cows drinking from the River Hipper, which, with artistic license, he paints tumbling through rapids as it flows from east to west, from the Rother to Holymoorside! On the low hill behind, on the right, is the unmistakable parish church, characterised by its crooked spire, with much of the visible town running down St. Mary's Gate to the Rother crossing. To the right on West Bars stands the imposing West House, home of the Maynard family, with Rose Hill peeping out behind it. Both are separated from the town by their private park and gardens while their lifestyle is reflected in the coach and horses travelling in from Baslow.

What is striking is the small size of the borough with its 950 houses crowded into just short of 300 acres, an area which had not increased since medieval times. Still primarily a market town trading in cattle, hides and grain, over the next thirty years it was to feel the impact of depression, following the Napoleonic wars, as the sally into iron-making collapsed, trade declined and the buildings deteriorated and fell into disrepair.

Sanitation, never a strong point, lacked investment and while the tanneries kept up some of their trade the smell of flesh rotting on skins awaiting treatment would have pervaded the hovels developing in the yards below Low Pavement.

1

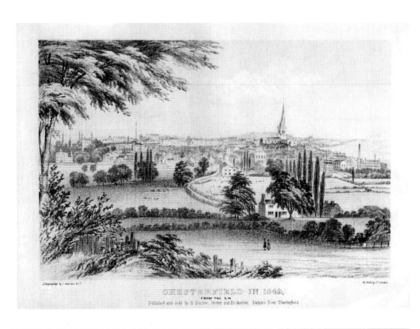

CHESTERFIELD IN 1843,
FROM THE S.W.
Published and Sold by R Barber, Printer and Bookseller, Packers Row, Chesterfield.

A later, turn-of-the-century, view of Queens Park - built on Maynard's Meadows

The Boating Lake, Queen's Park, Chesterfield.

A welcome change in fortune came with the entrepreneurial spirit of such as George Stephenson, Alfred Barnes and Charles Markham, bringing with them the stimulus of railways, coal mining and engineering. During the 1840s and 1850s Chesterfield felt the impact of its industrial revolution which became self-generating and saw the erection of new public and private buildings and the build up of pressures that finally burst the borough's old boundaries and ultimately expanded it to include what had all been neighbouring townships.

What the town looked like on the eve of this explosion has been captured in a delightful sepia coloured lithograph etched in 1849 by J. Newman & Co. of London and sold locally by Barnes the printer in Packers' Row. The artist has again chosen a view from the south west but has placed himself higher up Boythorpe hill, possibly near where the cemetery is today, so that more of the imposing buildings are depicted.

Again the setting for the scene is essentially rural with fields running down to *Maynard's Meadow* (which was not to become Queen's Park for another half century). To the east of Wheldon Lane, now only traceable in parts of Park Road, which led across a bridge into a yard below the market square is the large field used as a sports ground and occasionally for drills of the militia volunteers.

The town itself is still dominated by the twisted spire secure on the church of All Saints set on the small rise behind a row of poplar trees which hide tannery buildings off Lords Mill street. The houses run down the scarp of St. Mary's Gate with open crofts behind, on into Lord's Mill street culminating at Smith Holmes & Co's Spital Mill already on its last textile legs and ready to be taken over as Mason's tobacco works. Across the main road was the flour mill, which survived for a hundred and fifty years after the lithograph was produced and was only recently demolished.

On the far left of the engraving is West House with Rose Hill, still with its private gardens and orchards and room for a pack of harriers. The new union workhouse with its cupola, inspired by the Poor Law Amendment Act of 1834 and opened on Newbold Road in 1840, stands with the Board of Guardians' building alongside the tower of the newly built Holy Trinity church, soon to be the resting place of George Stephenson. Between these buildings towers the smoking chimney of some unidentified works, possibly a foundry sited in Whittington.

Slightly to the east, still on the horizon can be made out the flat-topped chimneys of the long Georgian terrace that still adds grace to Saltergate, while nearer to the church stands the home of the Durrant family with their considerable still open park land running down the northern scarp, out of view, to the Rother. This was the site taken by the old Royal Hospital in 1859 when the Durrant mansion was demolished.

To the west the town stopped at the boundary of the Rose Hill estate where the artist has drawn in the United Reform church erected in 1822 and the *Angel Inn* with a yard stretching right back to Saltergate. Further east, beyond the market place, still dominated by the old market hall (which was not replaced by the present building with its clock tower until 1857) can be seen the theatre in the yard of that name and the Municipal Hall, with its four large windows and arches at ground level, at the top of the ancient bowling green. At the south end of the green, hidden by the tree, was the House of Correction, a mixture of workhouse and punishment prison, while further east, on the northern thrust of a meander of the Hipper it is just possible to make out the water-powered silk mill. Another mill, possibly Holland's lace mill, stands on the edge of the sports field.

It was this, still confined borough, that had to accommodate a burgeoning population that doubled its size from seven to fourteen thousand in the next forty years as Chesterfield became a quasi-industrial town servicing the coal mines and iron works that sprang up mainly on its outskirts. The long burgess plots running down from the market to the river were soon crowded with slums that were to survive nearly until 1949 and much of the open ground disappeared under new buildings.

Today, it is hard to find a place on Boythorpe hill from which to see the town so crowded is the built up area. But a view from Park Road reveals the new town hall, the Georgian terrace chimneys, the mill-like multi-storeyed car park, the fortress police headquarters and the very new Vicar Lane development. The trees in Queen's Park hide the few unculverted parts of the river but the Church of St. Mary and All Saints stands unchanged on the town hill as it has for nearly eight centuries and may well stand for eight more.

The Coal Owner Member for Chesterfield

The story of Alfred Barnes of Ashgate

THE BARNES FAMILY of Ashgate, Chesterfield, were always innovators, at the forefront of technology. John Barnes, the yeoman whose family had acquired the first elements of the Ashgate estate in the sixteenth century not only had a large farm with a windmill crushing bones, some brought from the abattoirs of London, to turn them into fertiliser but by the 1750s was exploiting the coal seams of Barlow and making iron at Stonegravels.

One of his eight children, David, married Ellen Gorrell, and it was their only son, John Gorrell Barnes, who set the family on its way to further fortune. He married Elizabeth Taylor Clay, daughter of a well-breeched North Wingfield family and continued to live in Ashgate House, the family home commenced in 1647 but much extended by him.

Of their eight children, William, Henry and Charles set up a very successful shipping business in Liverpool. Charles went out to Australia to establish a similar business in Sydney and was joined for a short while by his brother Edmund. But Edmund did not take to the life down-under and returned to join in a partnership with his brother Alfred.

Alfred, born in 1823, was the youngest son of John Gorrell and his father thought it would serve him best to be trained as an engineer. To this end he was sent to the works of Robert Stephenson in Newcastle. He made good progress but this was checked when it was found that he had a weak heart. A more sedentary employment was proposed and he joined Todd Mather & Co. in Liverpool to become acquainted with business practice before, at the age of twenty three, being set up by his father to operate a colliery at Grassmoor just beyond the township of Hasland.

There had been coal mines at Grassmoor for nearly a century. Those at Winsick had been sunk by the Brocksopp family which had died out with the death of the spinster Mary Brocksopp, the only daughter of John Brocksopp, a farmer, colliery operator and ironmaster, in 1834. John Brocksopp had appointed his friend John Gorrell Barnes as his executor, and the young Mary, not perhaps realising the potential value of Birchill and Grasshill farms left them to her guardian.

It was on the 100 or so acres of these farms that the Grassmoor colliery was developed. Alfred was short of capital and recalls how on the first day the total output was taken away from the land-sales (for there was no railway connection) by an old woman with a donkey cart. Alfred must have been glad when Edmund joined him and brought in some more cash taking the capital up to £5,000.

The early years were not easy but the partnership made reasonable progress, and the brothers, who were close, felt secure enough to marry two sisters on the same day. Sadly Edmund died in 1870 just as the London coal market boomed and the Grassmoor Coal Co. started rapidly to increase its share of the market that had, for so long, been the preserve of the Clay Cross Coal and Iron Co. As the Top Hard seam of coal started to be worked out, a new shaft was sunk to the Blackshale seam 440 yards deep and the labour force rose to 3,000 producing 750,000 tons annually from the colliery, by then one of the largest in Derbyshire.

Pleased with the partnership's success Alfred, who had moved, with his wife Charlotte, and family, first from Ankerbold and then from Whitecotes, to the newly purchased Ashgate Lodge, across the road from the old house, and not in the original Barnes' estate, considered what best he could do for his four sons and two daughters. To protect them he converted the partnership in 1884 to a

6

limited liability company, the Barnes family holding the controlling share interest. As the boys reached maturity they joined the company, young Arthur, born in 1855, going on to become the chairman, Alfred Thomas, two years younger, qualifying as a mining engineer and being responsible for much of the underground work before becoming managing director, whilst Ernest Edmund, with a sales flare promoted the colliery's marketing

During the 1880s coal sales dipped as the economy entered a period of national depression but Alfred's foresight gave the company an unequalled boost. He had set up a London based sales force and risked the survival of the company by taking out the lease of railway waggons at the height of the depression. He was thus better placed than his competitors to take immediate advantage of the up-turn in the market when it came, clearing ten shillings a ton profit on 100,000 tons.

Throughout these later years of the century relationships with the railways and the nascent trade unions were not easy. The railway companies were attempting to exploit their near monopoly position by squeezing the individual coal owners. Alfred Barnes was more ready than many of his fellow colliery operators to see the value of combination to meet the strength of the railways and the miners' unions.

To this end he was instrumental in 1890 in setting up the Derbyshire, Nottinghamshire and Leicestershire Coal Owners' Association (later expanded to cover all the coal fields other than South Wales, Northumberland and Durham) and represented the coal owners in a number of negotiations with the railways and unions. Unlike Storrs-Smith of the Sheepbridge Company, but in line with the thinking of Charles Markham of the Staveley Company, he was opposed to the unionisation of his labour force and engaged in a long dispute when he threatened to dismiss men joining a union.

Unlike Markham, he turned away from local to national politics being elected as the Liberal M.P. for Chesterfield from 1880 to 1892 with a short break in 1885. In that year he was defeated by the Gladstonian Liberal Thomas Bayley who had pledged to support the miners' eight hour day bill (and was pettily charged with spitefully locking out men because he had lost) but regained the seat at the general election in the following year by the nail-biting margin of 114 votes.

But his commitment to the wider interests of the coal owners did not detract from his management of the Grassmoor Company. He was always ready to plough back profits, building coke ovens at the colliery, experimenting with electric lighting under-ground and always ensuring the screening and picking belts were of the latest design to provide the best customer service. The brickmaking machine produced 14,000 bricks a day providing all the colliery's needs and an ample supply for sale. And after a serious explosion at Parkhouse colliery, Danesmoor, he offered to finance the provision of safety-lamps entirely at the Company's expense, though other companies required a contribution from the men, but the colliers were reluctant to give up the use of candles they provided themselves, because the light was better.

Although he was such a shrewd business man he always retained something of his family's yeoman roots. He was a first class shot, handled a four-in-hand with panache and enjoyed a day's hunting with his four sons, stabling as he did 14 hunters and carriage horses at Ashgate.

Aged 67, Alfred died in 1901 leaving his sons to carry on the business. This they did during the difficult years leading up to the War and then through the period of manpower shortage and virulent absenteeism. The lock-outs of the early twenties and the General Strike soured relations between management and men but that did not stop Arthur Barnes from putting in place the arrangements for the first pit-head baths in Derbyshire opened by Ben Turner, the Minister for Mines at the end of 1929. This was one year after the Barnes family had put the company into voluntary liquidation, withdrawn their participation, and sold it to a newly formed company under the chairmanship of I.W.Lamonby.

The new Company built regenerative coke ovens and prospered during the Second World War but the colliery, over a hundred years old, was a relatively early victim of the closure programme of nationalisation. All that now remains is a solitary winding wheel set in its frame alongside Grassmoor business park.

And had not Edwin Barnes, one of Alfred sons, not successfully appealed to his fellow coal owners after the First World War for contributions to add another wing named Barnes Ward to the

Royal Hospital, the name and contribution of that innovative local family may have been entirely forgotten.

Charity Begins at Home

WHEN MRS ALEXANDER, at the end of the nineteenth century, wrote 'All things bright and beautiful' she was expressing a commonly held view that set 'The rich man in his castle, /The poor man at his gate,/ God made them, high and lowly,/ And ordered their estate.' But fortunately the rich men had a sense of conscience that encouraged them to give alms to the poor that were always with them.

The medieval gilds like those of the Blessed Mary, the Holy Cross and St. Helens, in Chesterfield all encouraged their members to make charitable bequests in their wills so as to alleviate the suffering of the poor. This work had also been underwritten by the monasteries but their removal from the scene in the 1530s left a gap in the welfare provision, diverting what little was available to alleviate the plight of elderly spinsters and widows who could no longer fend for themselves.

Despite his quarrels with the burgesses of Chesterfield, the Earl of Shrewsbury, Bess of Hardwick's husband, left money for the poor of Chesterfield, as did Gilbert Heathcote's widow. And so did Godfey Wolstenholm who in 1682 bequeathed the area of land known as poor folks fold (to the south of the spire church now a car park) to the burgesses so that the income could be given to the poor. With this bequest was coupled a house then tenanted by Elias Coates at a rent of £2 :10 shillings per year to boost the income.

His gift had been preceded by a bequest made in the 1668 will of George Taylor a wealthy burgess who had bought up the Durrant estate from the Alsops. Taylor directed that land should be

10

former almshouses on Newbold Road, Chesterfield

women in the workhouse, c 1890

bought 'near to the Moot Hall Orchard, (near to the town bowling green) in some open sweet street' and that six small houses should be built of stone and covered with slate, each with 'a garden spot about ten yards square'. He went on to provide a source of income for the inmates and a fund to finance young men wanting to start up in business.

No suitable land seems to have been found near the Moot Hall orchard by the Corporation, charged with administrating the fund,so the houses were built in Saltergate opposite what was soon to become the entrance to the Unitarian Chapel Sunday School. The houses were ranged pleasantly around an open square that allowed neighbours to look across at one another. Behind the houses the steam flour mill with its tall chimney was subsequently erected.

. The Corporation trustees paid, in 1827, a shilling a week to each inmate, provided a new gown each year, and contributed a shilling for coals. Ten years later responsibility for the alms houses was taken over from the Corporation by the Charity Commissioners. In 1861 the Duke of Devonshire, who was acquiring land in Chesterfield at this time, bought the site but sold it a year later to Francis Cooper together with an adjoining shop.

These purpose-built seventeenth century houses were fairly basic and after nearly two centuries of use were in serious need of replacement. Opportunity came when the trustees agreed to demolition so that the site could be redeveloped to accommodate eleven houses partially funded by the personal gift of the Rev John Boyers and the charities set up in the seventeenth and eighteenth centuries by Thomas Large, George Taylor and Sarah Rose with further monies coming from the Earl of Shrewsbury, Gill, the grocer, and many other Chesterfield tradesmen.

The new houses, eleven in all, each with three rooms, were built in 1875 again in the plan of a hollow square with an imposing entrance from Saltergate through gates mounted on high stone pillars. They were single storied, built of red brick with high decorative chimneys-stacks capped with fluted pots.

The new houses were soon occupied by ten indigent old ladies, two with daughters, while one was temporally empty early in 1881. In the first was Martha Elliott a widow of 85 who had been born in Retford and was an alms woman. With her lived her daughter of

58 who eked out a living as a tailoress. Next door was Phoebe Bellamy born and bred in Chesterfield who at 76 was a widow. Number 3 was empty, but another widow, Jane Nixon, a spry 82, who had started her days in Doncaster occupied number 4. The only elderly spinster was Frances Stevenson, a youthful 69, who had been a cook but had fallen on hard times. Facing Saltergate across the yard was the home of Hannah Mitchell a widow of 78 whose neighbour was another of the nine alms widows, Sarah Newbold, 80, also born in Chesterfield. The others came from farther afield, Jane Parker,72, came from Leicestershire, Elizabeth Clarke from Wessington and Mary Morris from Maidstone in Kent. With Mary Morris lived her daughter Alied Nuttal aged 48 who was blind and had to be supported by parish relief. Martha Boulder, a Chesterfield woman aged 78 lived in the last house abutting the street.

They were not required to attend religious services, as were the inmates of the Union Workhouse on Newbold Road but a census in 1898 shows that of the eleven then occupants, eight were dissenters and three Anglicans roughly reflecting the religious make up of the town.

Unfortunately we know little about how the townsfolk treated these poor people. They did receive eight shillings a week and a penny loaf of bread from the trustees and at least they were housed and dry. But did the school children running home from the national school in Soresby Street, or the newly opened National School on Durrant Road sprint a little faster past the railings on Saltergate fearing the old ladies in their down at heel gowns and bonnets were a coven of witches?

The 1875 alms houses protected the town's alms women for nearly another hundred years. But by the 1970s attitudes to the poor and needy had been fundamentally changed and it was decided to demolish the alms houses on Saltergate and provide 24 modern bungalows for elderly ladies at St. Helen's Court, Newbold Road.

Today the site of the old alms houses is unidentifiable under the central town car park. And the Anglican community have dropped singing that inappropriate verse from Mrs Alexander's otherwise timeless hymn.

Metamorphosis of a parsonage into a museum

T HE OLD WOMAN SLOWLY LOWERED herself on to the bench beside the church, resting her basket on the ground. She had been down to Bakewell market to sell some of the surplus eggs from the newly built parsonage and use the money to buy provisions. Her basket was heavy and, as she sat to recover her breath before continuing up the hill to the house of her master Christopher Plant, she turned over in her mind the strange talk she had heard about Beauchief Abbey being closed down.

The so-called parsonage house built of stone quarried locally from both sides of the Wye had been put up by Ralph Gell of Hopton and let to his steward Christopher Plant, who was responsible for collecting in the great tithes from as far afield as Taddington, Holmesfield and Chapel-en-le-Frith and storing them in the building described in the 1534 lease as the large 'wolle house..standing nigh'.

The Gells prospered as the lands seized from the monasteries came cheaply on to the market and by 1550 Ralph, already a skillful lawyer, had become the 'receiver-general and collector of farms, rents and profits' throughout the extensive parish of Bakewell. His lawyer son, Anthony and his brother Thomas, continued in their father's footsteps consolidating their land holdings and extending the parsonage house. Although Thomas's son, Sir John, played a prominent role in Derbyshire during the Civil War the family fortunes were already in decline.

After the lapse of some years the enlarged house passed

14

The Old Parsonage, Bakewell

through the marriage of a widow of the Gells to a branch of the Eyre family but during the eighteenth century it fell into decay and was bought cheaply by Sir Richard Arkwright. He converted it into a series of one-up one-down tenements for his Bakewell mill workers until the mill burned down in 1860.

The land and buildings were then sold off and slowly deteriorated into little more than slums despite some attempt in the early 1900s to restore the property. By 1955 it was seen as a potential health hazard fit only for demolition but fortunately the newly-formed Bakewell and District Historical Society stepped in and saved this fascinating building, one of the oldest non-ecclesiastical buildings in Bakewell, for posterity.

The volunteer members of this society have laboured over the last forty years, as funds would allow, to refurbish the building carefully restoring the roof and much of the internal partitioning. In the process they have revealed many of the characteristics of the materials used over the three hundred and fifty years of the original construction and its many adaptations. Most unusual in a relatively small domestic house is the garderobe, a lavatory shaft, running from the upstairs bedroom vertically alongside the fire place chimney, with its cleaning pit concealed behind a sliding stone.

To give a purpose to all this work the Society have converted the premises into an intimate museum open to the public, each of the rooms being devoted to the presentation of a wide range of social history themes and staffed by knowledgeable curators.

To the right of the entry porch (once a kitchen) is the old parlour now devoted to documents, drawings, photographs and some delightful models that trace the development of the house and its various uses. Right behind this room is the smaller buttery which has been part converted into a living representation of the wheelwright's workshop from Calver, while another part recalls an old Bakewell blacksmith's forge which has its bellows so wired up that they can artfully be pumped to make the hearth fire glow.

The essential centre of the original Tudor house was the so-called house place with its huge open fireplace complete with niches to keep the salt boxes dry. Here perhaps the most intriguing exhibits are the griddles for making Derbyshire oat-cakes and the slatted rack to hoist them aloft to cool out of the way of hopeful dogs and prying fingers.

Accessed from this room are Pitt's kitchen, Harrison's living room, the coal cellar and the scullery, named after their one-time occupants or their some-time usage. The kitchen is crammed with furniture and utensils of a century ago and provokes nostalgia amongst the senior citizens and cries of disbelief from the children. But it is the Harrison room that intrigues the children most containing as it does an incredible range of children's toys and games. The Harrisons were the last owners of the whole premises and the occupants of this seventeenth century addition, drawing rents from the lessees of the other tenements. The Society was very fortunate that one of them, an octogenarian, visited the museum and detailed how the family had lived in almost claustrophobic quarters.

Upstairs there is a further range of thematic rooms devoted to lace, sewing machines, Ashford black marble work, cameras, nineteenth and twentieth century samplers and a beguiling collection of authentic costumes ranging from Regency to the flappers of the twenties drawn from the professional and middle classes of Bakewell.

The climb from Bakewell is still as steep as it was for that Tudor woman servant but there is still a seat in the churchyard where you can catch your breath and look out at the town below. And making the rest of the climb to enjoy a couple of hours savouring the delights of a bygone age in the Old House Museum is well worth while.

The museum is open every day in the summer from 11 a.m. to 4 p.m. and in the autumn from 1.30 p.m. to 4 p.m. Admission: adults £2.50 children £1.

Look after the pence...

Early Banking in Chesterfield

NOW THAT CHESTERFIELD seems to have nearly as many banks and building societies as public houses it is hard to imagine the streets without any banks. But such was the situation well into the eighteenth century.

Banking in England goes back at least to the time of the Conquest when the Jews were the main bankers in the community. They lost ground to the Lombards (of Lombard Street) who in turn were replaced by the goldsmiths. The security of plate was one of the main functions of the nascent banking houses and it was from their goldsmiths' business that Coutts and Hoares moved into banking.

Valuables had long been deposited in the Tower of London for safekeeping but when Charles I seized £200,000 of gold and jewels the reliability of the Tower was thrown open to question, even though the King repaid the depositors. Some alternative seemed necessary and despite the opposition of the private London bankers William of Orange was pleased to charter the Bank of England in 1694 in exchange for a substantial loan to finance his wars against the French. The Bank had no monopoly of note issue but an Act of 1709 limiting the right of issue only to those houses with fewer than six persons effectively gave the Bank a considerably advantage. A number of private banks did start up but the majority of them went to the wall in the financial crisis of 1793. This collapse led to private banks cutting back on issuing notes while allowing customers to draw cheques on the bank instead. But still there were no joint stock banks with stockholders with a limited liability.

The merchants of Chesterfield had watched developments with interest and in 1808 they welcomed Crompton and Newton & Co, who had operated a bank in Derby City from around 1685, when they opened their bank named the Scarsdale and High Peak Bank, at the south west corner of the Shambles (where the Abbey National building society is today). By the 1830s they had moved to a house at the end of Glumangate, only moving again by expanding into a fine new building taking in part of the Star Inn site in 1894 and then extending further when the Angel was demolished in 1926.

The directors of the branch were John Crompton and Gilbert Crompton, (descendants of Abraham Crompton who had started the business in Derby), John Bell Crompton, John Leaper Newton, William Newton, and William Waller a Chesterfield solicitor, and uncle of another William Waller who became town clerk in 1818. John Crompton was the son of Samuel Crompton and father of John Bell Crompton so the family ties were close. Gilbert Crompton went on to be mayor of the Borough on four occasions between 1823 and 1840.

Their banking business was rather different from modern day banking being principally concerned with the receiving of deposits which tended to be used to finance investments away from the town. Current accounts were rare, so much so that by the end of the first year there were only eighteen personal accounts, one of them being held by the Duke of Devonshire. The number of accounts grew slowly, seven being added in 1809, that of Sir Thomas Hunloke being among them, and it was not until three years later that the Chesterfield Corporation opened an account.

The accounts books for these early years highlight how much the value of the currency has been affected by inflation, all the records being kept to the farthing (a quarter of a penny when there were 240 pennies to the pound). Nevertheless the holdings in specie were equally surprising. At the end of the first week the new branch held £1950 in gold, £50 in silver, £1590 in bank notes and £1465 in country notes. The safe at the bank must have been deemed inadequate for a few years later the records show that Mr Crompton was keeping £11,000 in gold, silver and notes for the bank at his house in Holywell Street.

What the hours of business were are uncertain but closure

was limited only to Good Friday and Christmas Day though the coronation of George IV in 1821 led to a closed day as did the funeral of one of the partner's wives.

The Crompton bank issued notes and this distinguished them from the other private banks founded in Chesterfield by Isaac Wilkinson and his family, Jebb, Slater and Malkin.

Banking was still something of an esoteric art in the provinces until the Bank of England's note-issuing monopoly was finally broken in 1826 and the formation of joint stock banks with limited shareholders' liability was permitted by the Act of 1833. Overnight banks mushroomed, a hundred new joint stock banks being founded in the first year.

By that date John Coller had a bank on Packers Row and Maltby and Robinson in New Square were a small bank which like Crompton's issued notes. But the new banking measure caused some concern in Chesterfield, the locals fearing that the control of banking, and hence the availability of new money for investment in the developing industries would be centred on London. To challenge any such move a meeting was called at the Angel Inn where it was agreed to form the Chesterfield Joint Stock Banking Company the name being modified to the Chesterfield and North Derbyshire Banking Company, at its inauguration in 1834. The new bank had a nominal capital of £250,000 of which £23,280 was subscribed by the opening. A number of local worthies were the directors, amongst them William Robinson and John Gorell Barnes, with George Walker as the branch manager.

John Barnes took the opportunity of the new note issue when he needed to send money to Mary Brocksopp, his ward in Cheltenham. There had been thefts from the post so Barnes cut a note in half sending the second half by post only when Mary confirmed she had received the first part.

Saving by the less fortunate was a matter of concern to many of the non-conformist traders and it was to encourage such saving that a Savings Bank with nine trustees, with Gilbert Crompton as Treasurer, was established in 1816 and initial deposits of nine shillings and sixpence, (48p). It was much patronised by the growing number of self-help friendly societies though there must have occasionally been long queues, the branch in Vicar Lane only being open on Saturdays from 2p.m. for an hour and a half. But it was a huge success and filled a much felt need.

By the 1870s banks were finding it necessary to grow larger by consolidation of interests. Crompton and Newton joined with Evans' Bank (also founded in Derby in 1771) to form Crompton and Evans' Union Bank in 1877. There was a further merger between the new bank and the Chesterfield & North Derbyshire in 1878 which in turn was acquired by Parr's Bank at the start of the First World War. In its turn Parr's was taken over by the National Westminster Bank.

Further amalgamations saw the emergence of the big five and then the movement of building societies into banking. The whole scale of the operation changed over time and it's unlikely that any branch manager will ever be asked to keep under his bed the sort of cash held by Mr Crompton in his house in Holywell Street.

A Century of Industry in Chesterfield, 1898-1998

IN 1836 TWO LETTERS signed 'Mercator' appeared in the *North Derbyshire Chronicle* which reviewed at length the economic condition of Chesterfield and asked 'Why does Chesterfield with all its natural advantages remain poor and unimportant while other towns in all parts of the kingdom, without such advantages, have grown and continue to grow in wealth and importance?' The writer concluded it was because of a want of energy and skill in the application of capital.

But such a cynical approach turned out to be unwarranted for Mercator did not give a proper weight to the impact railways were to have opening the almost land-locked town, served as it was by three railway stations, to markets in London and world wide. The canal link to Stockwith had been interrupted and then finally cut by the collapse of the Norwood Tunnel in 1908 and no longer had any commercial role to play. It had, however, played its part in establishing, in the 1850s and 60s, the Sheepbridge and Staveley Coal and Iron limited liability companies, the opening of William Oliver, the engineering company, and Edward Eastgate's railway wagon building works. New collieries were sunk almost annually so that by

sweetmakers at Trebor Sharps factory

Processing hides at Clayton's tannery

the end of the first decade of the twentieth century Chesterfield which a hundred years earlier had been little more than a small market town with industrial overtones had become a borough where barely one and a half percent of males were engaged in agriculture but 27 percent of the male labour force was engaged in mining, a number which was to reach over 50 per cent by 1929.

Pits at Brampton, Boythorpe and Whittington, outside the borough, but underpinning its economy, not only supplied the local iron manufacturing trades but were breaking into the London domestic coal market. The most successful in this enterprise were the collieries of the Clay Cross Company, closely followed by the Sheepbridge and the Staveley companies so that by the late 1870s over 80,000 tons of coal was transported from Derbyshire to London by the Midland railway in a single month. These collieries would be the big employers for most of the century, the Markham pits peaking to employ 2,670 men, Grassmoor 1,600, Ireland 1,300 and Williamthorpe over a thousand.

The coal industry was far from free-standing, both the Sheepbridge and Staveley companies having close association with iron manufacture and engineering. Charles Markham, a director of the Staveley company, bought out Oliver's in 1889, taking over the Broad Oaks Works and developing it to become a principal manufacturer of pit winding gear and later turbines and tunnelling shield equipment. Fifteen years earlier the Plowright brothers had established a works at Brampton also servicing the burgeoning coal mining industry while in the early 1900s Bryan Donkin, long established in London, moved to Chesterfield to enter the gas valve and governor market and Chesterfield Tubes opened up its seamless steel and high tensile alloy tube and cylinder works so that on the eve of the First World War 16 percent of employed males worked in the metal and engineering sector.

These industries were hot and dusty and the pubs did well, adequately supplied as they were by the town's three breweries: Scarsdale, Old Brampton and Chesterfield. But by the middle of the century the local breweries were being taken over by the national companies. Mansfield Breweries bought out and closed the Chesterfield plant in 1935 and the other two followed suit in the 1950s and 60s terminating the long tradition once praised by Celia

Fiennes. Only the Chesterfield plant was saved, the site being adapted for sweet making by Trebor (a south of England based company) now owned by the Bassett Group.

The other 'leisure industry', tobacco manufacture, conducted at Mason's works in Spital had seemed destined to compete successfully with Players at Nottingham but the customers were not loyal to 'Cropper' cigarettes and the company was wound up in 1907.

Not all the town's industries were in such difficult straits but World War I provided a useful fillip to its industries. Although the productivity of the mines fell, after an initial decline, the gross production rose and the demand for armaments boosted the profitability of the engineering companies. Similarly stimulated was Robinson and Sons Ltd., which had been founded in 1839 and had benefited from the demand for medical dressings in the Crimea war and enlarged its output of textile medical supplies and packaging between 1914 and 1918.

The other traditional textile industries, stocking knitting (last represented by Crow and Son on High Street), silk and lace manufacture had already disappeared soon after the turn of the century and the staple of tanning, leather ware and boot manufacture was kept alive only by Harrisons, making boots in the old silk mill, Slack's producing tan leather, sod and cod oils at the works at the end of Lord's Mill Street and Clayton's. Only Clayton's, which had employed over a hundred making leather harnesses, survived after the World War II, curtailed in manpower but meeting the demands of a prosperous niche market requiring specialist leathers.

It was not the availablity of markets but rather the supply of labour and cheap power that brought Dema Glass to Chesterfield in World War I, to pick up again the industry made famous by Richard Dixon of Whittington Hall. This innovation was followed in 1923, by a subsidiary of British Thompson Houston, making glass parts for electric lamps and then by its neighbouring factory, Lamp Caps, making the associated brass parts. All these struggled commercially in the 1980s and only barely survived, Dema, following a management buy out, specialising in producing high class table glass ware.

Surprisingly the period between the Wars, which had devastated the coal based economies of South Wales and Durham,

The Bryan Donkin Works from the Air.

Brian Donkin & Co

Pearson's pottery works

had relatively little impact on the economy of Chesterfield. Whilst the demand for coal suffered some temporary setbacks, the London domestic market remained buoyant and the Staveley Coal and Iron Company, specialising in the supply of spun pipes for gas and sanitation, making it the second largest pipe manufacturer in the country, retained a strong order book which resulted in the unemployed manpower of Staveley falling from 9 percent in 1933 to only two percent in 1939, while that at Bolsover hovered around 15 percent throughout the decade.

The years of national economic depression ended with rearmament and the World War II saw a major change in the pattern of the employment of women, 23 percent of whom, for the first three decades, found paid work in domestic service. World War II saw the number of females employed in engineering rise tenfold and in metal manufacture 250 times to a total of 770 women. At the end of the war women left many of these industries as men returned but the range of employment open to females remained enlarged, the Robinson and Son labour force running at around 3,500 mainly women, and the significance of the domestic service sector was forever eroded.

The post-war period with its incidence of nationalisation in coal, iron and steel, saw considerable new investment in the old heavy industries and burgeoning of new industries to meet the changes brought about by the internal combustion engine: Sheepbridge Stokes making centrifuged cylinder liners and George Kenning and Sons fuel and motor car distribution service contributing to the local economy are good examples.

This period also saw the extension of the chemical industry based on coal product refining. The low temperature carbonisation plant started by the Coalite Chemical Company in the 1930s at Bolsover to manufacture smokeless fuel and coal chemical derivatives expanded its activities and the old coke ovens of Grassmoor and Hardwick collieries were replaced by a state of the art carbonisation plant on the old Avenue colliery site which not only produced 1,400 tons of domestic and industrial coke daily but fed 27 million cubic feet of gas into the town's gas supply. This gas had to find a new use when natural North Sea gas displaced it for domestic use.

Such changes in the sources of supply affected other

27

industries and by the 1970s and '80s the effects of increasing national and international competition were becoming apparent. New machines produced more with less manpower and the stories in the Derbyshire Times were increasingly of redundancies at Bryan Donkin's, Tube Investments, Robert Hyde's, the steel founders, Robinson and Son (who in the 1980s closed their Holme Brook works and weaving sheds, sold Spire Transport and closed down the subsidiary J.J. Blow, manufactures of dairy equipment from 1917). Pearson's, the only remaining earthenware pottery, already hit by the substitution of glass ware for preserves, ran into financial difficulties and was only just saved and kept in production on a reduced scale. The demand for iron declined and only Staveley's chemical subsidiary kept the name alive (until it was taken over by the French based company, Rhone-Poulenc) the foundry business becoming only a shadow of its former self. The Sheepbridge Company similarly saw the demise of its iron making plant, its sortie into diversified engineering industries ending with the buy-out by the G.K.N. Group in 1979 leaving only a small G.K.N. Sheepbridge Stokes unit making cylinder liners on what has become the Sheepbridge trading estate, now the home of widely diversified manufactures. Others adapted, the Birtley Engineering Company turning from servicing the coal industry to more general minerals handling and water treatment.

The final blow to the heavy industries and their associated suppliers came in the early 1990s with the abrupt closure of all the remaining deep coal mines in north Derbyshire. But this was not to be the end of coal extraction, open-cast coal mining becoming an increasingly important industry, though a small employer, with 45 men on sites such as Poolsbrook and Duckmanton winning 200,000 tons, while restoring earlier deep mining pollution. Greenfield sites at Barrow Hill, Hall Lane, Breck and possibly Stainsby may see coal extraction running on into the next century.

The collapse of the heavy industries did not affect the prosperity of the town as much as may have been expected. During the early 1960s the national policy of redistributing the civil service had led to the opening of the Accountant General's Post Office Pensions service in Chesterfield. By the 1990s the Royal Mail services had become a major employer of over 2,750 people, with a new building, Rowland Hill House, on Boythorpe Road and a replacement for the original Chetwyn House being erected at West Bars.

At the same time new light industries in the electronics, automotive and very diverse fields were opening up on the half dozen trading estates in the district: Chesterfelt, making roofing felt, Permic, making marine safety equipment, Flogates, processing refractories and ironmaking control gear, Kiss Fashions, making leisure wear are but a few examples. Software designers have mushroomed and plastics manufactures have edged out more traditional materials. Most of the firms employed fewer than fifty people but their turnovers were of high value. The number of self employed rose rapidly in north Derbyshire, rising from 16,000 in 1990 to 21,000 seven years later. And in the High Street the service industries, financial advisers, insurance companies and building societies filled the shops left empty by Woodhead's, Turner's and J.K.Swallow and many more made empty by the new supermarket stores opened on the perimeter of the town.

Even the cattle market has become a retail trading site. So what would Mercator write in 1999? Would he marvel at how the heavy industry of Chesterfield thrived but declined during the century? And what would he see as the prospects for Chesterfield? Is the Hipper to house another Silicon Valley?

Sir Francis Legatt Chantrey

Artist and Sculptor of exquisite delicacy

O N A COLD NOVEMBER DAY a grocer's errand boy stopped to gaze at the fascinating carvings exhibited in the shop of the carver named Ramsey, in Sheffield, and realised that what he wanted more than anything in the world was to produce work like that.

The boy was young Frankie Chantrey, the sixteen year old son of a farmer and carpenter born in Jordanthorpe, Norton, in 1781. His wish was granted when he was apprenticed for seven years to Ramsey.

His talent as an artist was quickly recognised and encouraged by the mezzotint engraver J. Raphael Smith who frequented Ramsey's shop. Ramsey became a little jealous of Chantrey's ability and was more discouraging but Chantrey struggled on producing drawings, portraits and secretly practising sculpture.

He was taught oil painting by Samuel James and so good was his work that he was soon able to attract paid commissions and had no difficulty in buying himself out of the last two years of apprenticeship with Ramsey. Among his first sales were those to the file makers, Rhodes, Bramall and Jackson his portraits commanding a fee of five guineas.

To further his art he went to the Royal Academy in 1802 where he studied for a short time though not formally admitted as a student. Two years later his first picture, of his uncle, D. Wale, was hung at the Royal Academy.

Although he spent much of the rest of his life in London he never lost his Derbyshire accent and was always a little rough in manner and speech. The loss of his hair in early life through a fever contracted during a short stay in Ireland distracted from the composure of his face. But he was not a man of 'artistic temperament' always having a ready humour, (excelling as a mimic), being a good host and enjoying a good dinner and nothing more than a good day fishing or shooting. His prowess as a shot being immortalised when he killed a brace of woodcocks with one shot and depicted the kill in a beautiful carving.

From 1804 he devoted all his talent to sculpture, particularly bust portraiture. His first commission, executed in marble, was of the Rev. Wilkinson erected in the parish church at Sheffield. Other Sheffield friends patronised him and his financial worries were finally resolved on the marriage to Miss Wale, his cousin, who brought a dowry in land of £10,000.

The couple took up residence in Pimlico and Chantrey crowned his progress by winning the competition for the Guildhall statue of George III. Success followed success and by 1809 he had no fewer than six busts exhibited at the Academy. Following a commission of a bust of the president of the R.A. and the bust of the artist Raphael Smith that enchantingly catches the expression of the deaf listener Chantrey, received commissions worth over £12,000.

With his wife he made a brief tour through the Pennines, in 1806, recording the beauty and the comic incidents of the journey in a pencil sketch book and in 1814 visited the great collection at the Louvre, where he met Canova. This acquaintance was renewed when the couple went to Italy, Chantrey visiting Canova's gallery and taking the opportunity to select and buy Carrara marble. While, to ensure the quality of his casting in bronze, he operated his own foundry.

The catalogue of his busts and statues reads like a list of the great and famous: Thomas Munro, Wellington, the equestrian George IV (in Trafalgar Square), William Pitt, Walter Scott, Robert Peel, Joseph Banks, James Watt, and so many others.

His reputation, widely acclaimed, was sealed with full membership of the Royal Academy in 1818 and a knighthood from William IV, in 1835, honourary degrees at Oxford and Cambridge and a Fellowship of the Royal Society.

Whilst his professional reputation was established in his portraiture in stone from life, his artistic genius is found in his statuary of children that incorporates an incredible tenderness. The sleeping children, in Lichfield Cathedral, exemplify this talent as does the young Lady Louisa Russell with a dove, at Woburn.

Unfortunately the couple had no children and in his will

Chantrey provided for the reversion of his £150,000 estate, after the death of his widow, to the Royal Academy to set up the Chantrey Bequest destined to establish a collection of paintings and sculptures executed by artists resident in Britain at the time the work was executed.

His death came suddenly towards the end of November 1841, forty six years after the lonely errand boy had gazed so longingly at the carvings in Ramsey's shop window. He was laid to rest, in a tomb of his own design, in Norton, the parish of his birth.

Rope making in North Derbyshire

ODDLY, WHEN DANIEL DEFOE visited north Derbyshire at the beginning of the eighteenth century he was so preoccupied with denigrating the Wonders of the Peak that he made no mention of the long-term industry carried out in the dark reaches of Peak Cavern at Castleton. Unless, which seems unlikely, there was a short break in that industry during the period of his visit.

A later German visitor, Karl Moritz, who made a walking tour of the district in 1786 did, however, make a brief reference to the subterranean workers who were resting, it being Sunday, outside their pitiful huts. Their wheels and industrial equipment reminded him of the continuously rotating wheel of the mythical king Ixion and the incessant labour of Danaides never able to fill her leaking pitchers.

The industry in question was rope making which can be traced back to the building of the Egyptian pyramids and was carried on for at least 400 years in Peak Cavern before being abandoned at this site in the early 1960s. When Farey carried out his survey of agriculture and industry at the beginning of the nineteenth century he found rope making at Ashover, Bakewell, Brampton, Castleton and Hope in north Derbyshire and eight other places in the south of the County.

The local demand for ropes came first from farmers who needed tethers and halters for animals and to lash loads of fuel and fodder while they were moved on carts. And this demand was supplemented quickly by the lead miners who required much longer ropes to haul mineral out of the mines. As mines grew deeper with the sinking first of bell pits and then mine shafts to win coal and iron the need for stronger and longer ropes grew. And there was demand

from the canal longboat men for tow ropes and from brewers, while the increasing use of sash windows required a supply of narrow diameter sash cord.

Despite the increasing demand that came with industrialisation the method of making and the materials used in the manufacture process varied very little until the need for great strength led to the substitution of wire for hemp.

Hemp rope, the traditional manufacture, was made from a variety of botanically unrelated plants that were loosely referred to in the industry as hemp and today may come from Manila, India or more likely Poland or Italy. True hemp, *cannibis sativa*, was not widely grown locally but some was available along with flax and sisal to supply the coarse textile and rope making manufacturers.

As a crop hemp was grown in close rows to produce longish straight fibres which when harvested were processed, rather as flax is processed, by retting, bleaching and scutching. The separated fibres were then spun into yarns which in turn were twisted into cords before being laid into ropes.

It was this laying process that demanded a long even-surfaced area along which the pair of rope makers could walk. The method used involved hooking the cords, which are wound on bobbins, through a compression tube on to a revolving disc, or flyer. As the rope was laid the rope maker walked away from the flyer feeding in the yarn carried along by the bobbin carrier: the maximum length of the rope, without splicing, being determined by the length of the rope walk. Some of these were nearly 400 yards long but more usually half that length and while some were covered over, permitting all weather production, others were open to the elements.

It was this natural covering provided in the Peak Cavern that made the site so attractive and although the entrance cavern is restricted in depth, the cavern beyond is vast and its magnitude outweighs the need for artificial lighting so allowing it to outlive all the other rope making sites in north Derbyshire. There was little profit in the trade and the workers lived a wretched life, living underground for long periods together. Croston, walking through the Peak in 1868, found them with their machines and noise an unwelcome presence in so otherwise impressive a natural feature.

In contrast the site at Ashover was in the open fields, below the Rattle, and was operated in 1835 by the partnership of John and Joseph Twig. Its location can still be discerned in the field layout pattern. While this Ashover site was essentially rural that in Chesterfield was on the edge of the town running on the north side of Saltergate from Thorten Yard, on the opposite side of the road to and roughly midway between Holywell House and the old Royal hospital, nearly to Union Walk, a distance of about 150 yards.

The history of this site is shrouded for, though five rope makers are listed in the 1835 trade directory none seems to be identifiable to the Holywell Street rope walk, but it might have been worked by John Newton whose business was on Saltergate. The other four rope makers or rope traders in Chesterfield were in the Market Place and Packer's Row, while two named Wilkinson had businesses in Spa Lane and Stonegravels.

By 1884 the Holywell Street rope works had been taken over by a Robert Strachen who had learned his trade apprenticed for five years at Craven's Sunderland rope works and had moved to Chesterfield to set up his own business. He lived on the premises and

36

personally overlooked the rope making work, though much of his time was spent as a travelling salesman.

The principal building on the site consisted of a low pantile roofed shed standing on brick pillars which stretched the length of the plot and could be used in all weathers for making twine and light rope. Alongside ran another walk for making heavier ropes of manila, sisal and hemp. But the industry did not take a firm hold and soon after the turn of the century the works closed.

After the Strachens gave up, rope making was taken over by the Eyres on their neighbouring site and the work continued when Rylands acquired the business in 1928. Rope continued to be made until the early 1960s on a relocated rope walk on part of the site now occupied by the Jackson warehouse. In the post war years the demand for twine and rope declined and rope making ceased to be an occupation pursued anywhere in north east Derbyshire. Its demise has left only barely discernible vestigial clues as to where there had once been a thriving industry.

Silken Threads to the Past

BEFORE THE RIVER HIPPER was canalised alongside Queen's Park it swung in towards the town in a great meander. There, alongside what is now Markham Road, was a vacant patch of land liable to flooding which was leased to Joseph Burbeck and Abraham Staveley, two respected Chesterfield dyers.

Early in the 18th century it was sub-let to one Joseph Jebb, a hosier and borough alderman so that he could build a fulling mill powered by the stream. In fact, the hey-day of the woollen trade was already over but, though the fulling mill was less used, the pond provided a popular source of entertainment when nagging wives were treated to an early bath using the bank-side ducking stool.

Eventually the under-used mill itself attracted the interest of Philip Clowes. He saw the possibility of converting it to spin silk thread using the process known as silk 'throwing' and sometime in the mid-century Clowes introduced silk-throwing to Chesterfield, extending his lease of the mill when the Burbeck and Staveley lease ended in 1792.

Spinning and weaving silk had been a closely guarded Italian secret (gleaned from the Chinese) until the Lombe brothers, by the devious use of secret agents, patented their machine designs and built three spinning engines at Derby in 1771. Silk became fashionable and was not only used to make dress lengths for ladies but also coats and breeches for men and stockings for all those who could afford them.

It was this great pressure of demand which had stimulated Clowes to action and its continuation later persuaded the Tucker family to acquire the mill sometime before 1790 when Clowes himself

The old silk mill

a modern silk weaving demonstration

retired.

As a source of employment the mill was of substantial importance to the town providing work for 73 hands, mostly women and children and a few men. The majority of these lived within a short walking distance of the mill, crowded into the hovels grouped in the yards that stretched down from Beetwell Street to the river: Silk Mill Yard, Castle Yard, Brown's Yard, Spread Eagle Yard and along Church Alley to Lord's Mill Street.

The skilled doublers lived closest to the mill and the winders a little further away, while the only man living in Silk Mill Yard was Tucker, the owner, all the rest being women and children.

It was common for whole families to be connected with the trade, daughters following mothers into the factory. And, as befitted so important a work-place, it was amongst the highest rated businesses in the Borough.

What the working conditions were like can only be imagined, especially for the children whose little hands were needed to thread machines in inaccessible places. The water wheel would have creaked and groaned and the flow of water under the mill would have made it a chilly work-place in winter. In the later years this natural power was replaced by steam to make the mill less dependent on the vagaries of the weather.

But fashions changed rapidly after the Great Exhibition and within ten years employment levels had plummeted. Just twenty people had full-time employment in 1861. The future of silk spinning in the town was bleak and the Tuckers closed the mill around 1876.

It lay idle for a while and reverted to the Hoole family when George Tucker, who had inherited the property, could not pay the mortgage dues.

The future of the old four-storied building with its well-known silhouette marking the end of the town was now much less exotic. For a while it housed a fishing-tackle manufacturer, until James Hoole sold it, along with the Old House, to James Bradley.

Bradley was the proprietor of the Hipper Chemical Works and although the mill still had its 'dam, weirs, shuttles, goights,and appurtenances, thereto belonging' he did not use it for chemical manufacturing. Instead he let the property to a lamp-wick manufacturer named Barnes.

It was home to this industry for about twenty years before being leased to John Harrison & Son, boot and shoe manufacturers. It is their large sign on the side of the building that most older Chesterfeldians will remember.

The building steadily decayed and then, when the Corporation decided to widen Markham Road, it was bought and finally unceremoniously pulled down in 1967.

The old ducking-pond had been filled during the 1880s and the only thread, until the mid-1990s, linking this fragment of Chesterfield with the warp of its textile past, when frame-knitters, lace and net makers and silk throwers crowded the market place on Saturday evenings, was a sad length of wall alongside Markham Road and a barely traceable outline of the old goyt and pond. Even those vestigial remains have now been bulldozed away to site the new retail Ravenshead retail park leaving the Old Silk Mill as a fanciful memory.

The Growth of Chesterfield Town Hall

T HE TOWN HALL HASN'T ALWAYS BEEN the centre of civic administration. The everyday life of the inhabitants of Chesterfield in the England of Elizabeth I were much more conditioned by the decisions of the Vestry and the Manorial Court than the goings-on of the Corporation. And matters didn't change much over the next two hundred and fifty years.

The Vestry was the body which had no formal constitution comprised of the vicar and church wardens, and was responsible for the maintenance of the parish church of St Mary and All Saints. Its members were elected within the ecclesiastical parish, which was then far more extensive than the Borough. Over the years it had had its responsibilities extended to include the maintenance of the roads, the welfare of the poor and the keeping of the peace. And to discharge these duties the Vestry each year appointed one of the parishioners to be the Surveyor of the Highways and another the Overseer of the Poor, regardless of their past experience or suitability for the office.

The manorial court of the Lord of the Manor (who in Chesterfield changed fairly frequently until finally in the eighteenth and nineteenth century was one of the Dukes of Newcastle, Portland or Devonshire), meanwhile controlled a different range of public affairs. The most important was the peaceful operation of the market, and more mundane the keeping the town's streets free of gross obstruction from refuse, decaying animal remains, slops and worse.

The old police and fire station

Its much older responsibility for what crops should be planted, and when, in each of the open fields had declined as the open fields, were enclosed.

Meanwhile the Corporation, given its full status by the charter granted in 1598, seems in comparison to have played little part in the administration of the Borough. In its early years it was a self-perpetuating body drawing its membership from those who qualified as burgesses by owning a burgess plot of land. Its income came from lands and property given to the town primarily to generate income for charitable works, including the funding for needy apprentices and the provision of a grammar school. The school for a while was shamefully neglected, but funding never seems to have been short for the annual feasts of the worshipful members.

To administer the funds the council found it necessary to meet only twice a year assembling at the Council House built close to the Bowling Green on South Street in 1620. Over the years this building must have become unsuitable for meetings, for forty years later we find the Corporation leasing the Moot Hall from Viscount Mansfield, who reserved one of its rooms for the use of the manorial courts of Chesterfield and the Hundred of Scarsdale. It was this body that had obtained, in 1675, the license from the Lord of the Manor to build a covered market hall, raised on pillars, and, when it had decayed, its later replacement in 1764. This old Moot Hall had been built of timber and brick by William Soresby, the steward of the Countess of Oxford, one of the lords of the manor, to the north east of the market hall (where the HSBC bank now stands).

By 1787 the council was looking for yet another new home and was pleased occasionally to make use of the new town hall built at the end of Glumangate, probably to replace the old Moot Hall, instead of meeting, as it regularly did, in one of the town's many inns. The new building provided space on the ground floor for cells to imprison offenders awaiting trial and a courtroom for the Justices of the Peace as well as a hall for the quarterly meetings of the manorial court. It was a stylish building commended by Viscount Torrington on his tour through Derbyshire in 1789.

This building, private offices and inns, served two generations of councillors but by the 1840s, when the future of the theatre in Theatre Yard was uncertain, the council (together with the trustees of the Mechanics' Institute, also looking for new premises) cast covetous eyes on the conversion of the theatre to offices. (Does anything change?)

The forecast cost was however too high and while the council managed their twice a year meetings in their part time solicitor-town -clerk's private office they cast around for a new site. After some prevarication, when they turned down the Duke of Devonshire's offer of a building on Glumangate, they finally built a new Council House, completed by 1850, at the end of Beetwell Street and South Street (where the public library now stands).

By this time local government was changing and as Chesterfield industrialised the pressure was on for re-organisation. The Vestry had already unloaded its responsibility for the maintenance of the roads to a Highways Board, as such boards, to organise essential public services, became the accepted form of municipal management. And reform of the poor law had started in the 1830s with responsibility being taken over by the new Board of Guardians. The Cemetery Board tackled the increasing problem of limited burial space while the new school boards grappled with primary education. Meanwhile the Corporation continued to meet just twice a year electing its twelve members and four aldermen who

44

together, each year, elected the mayor.

The Borough in 1861 excluded the surrounding townships of Hasland, Brimington, Brampton and Whittington and still had fewer than ten thousand inhabitants. Into the eighties and nineties the problems of overcrowding in the Yards below Low Pavement and the disposal of sewage became overpowering and expansion of the Borough by incorporation of surrounding authorities became inevitable. Such absorption was strongly resisted and it was not until the 1890s that the Borough made its first boundary break-out, a process only completed by 1920 or even 1974.

As the Borough grew so did the need to accommodate the administration. Beetwell Street Town Hall was extended and provision was made to house the Borough's two fire engines. But again the hall soon became too small and the Council relocated its now quarterly meetings to the Stephenson Memorial building. This had been purchased in 1889 from the original owners when they had been unable to continue financing it.

By the turn of the century local government had become a growth industry. From the Municipal Corporations Act of 1835, through all the public health and educational acts, the responsibilities of the Council expanded. Party politics had hardly applied but between the Wars the elections started to be fought on party lines. With the series of housing acts, aimed at clearing away the hateful slums of places like the Dog Kennels, the work of the Council and their officials escalated.

By the 1930s civic pride and necessity warranted the purchase of the Rose Hill estate, the carrying through of Knifesmiths Gate into the gardens and the building of a prestigious town hall designed by Bradshaw, Gass and Hope (whose Irish Stormont building design echoes Chesterfield's). The new civic centre, opened in 1938 by the Duchess of Devonshire, was set off by the Shentall Gardens. At the same time the Borough's war memorial to the fallen of the two World Wars was re-sited outside the Town Hall from its former location alongside the parish church.

At St Mary's the wardens continue to meet, now only responsible for the care of the church, while the business of the Corporation is conducted from Rose Hill until the Council out-grows its accommodation and decides it is time to move yet again.

A Christmas Tragedy

PERHAPS THE MOST CENTRAL of the Chesterfield cinema-theatres was the short-lived Palace situated behind Burlington Street, with an entrance next to Mr Dale's, the ironmongers' shop in Church Street.

This was open, just a fortnight after the Skating Rink, on 25th September, 1909, boasting in its first advertisement "that while it was not gorgeous and lacked a wonderful entrance, it was complete inside with every comfort and tip-up seats throughout".

Unfortunately no records have survived to indicate whether the building was purpose built or was converted from other earlier usage, but the latter is more likely.

Towards the end of the Edwardian period cinemas were replacing live theatres as the principal places of mass entertainment and in Chesterfield the first building used solely for showing films was the Central Hall, a converted chapel in Brampton, opened in 1907 and soon renamed The Coliseum.

So successful was it that a second theatre, The Palace, was opened not solely for 'animated pictures' but rather for a mixed cinema and live show entertainment, interlinking the silent films with such acts as The Bohemians, instrumentalists and comedians.

The shows were held each weekday night, with children's matinees on Friday evenings and on Saturdays but no indication was given in these early years of what the titles of the films would be, let alone whom they starred. Nor was there any way of knowing whether the show had been good, bad or indifferent without attending, for the local newspaper did not yet have a film critic.

Not that there was any lack of drama, each sequence being enhanced by the latest effects machine, 'which faithfully reproduced the noise and bustle of the real life' portrayed on the screen, while Bertram Brennan, 'Derbyshire's premiere pianist', not only entertained but also musically heightened the heart-rending pathos.

Threepence secured a seat in the pit, a tanner (5p) a place in the pit stalls and a bob (10p) the luxury of the balcony. The Palace was well patronised. Entertainment tax at one and a half pence on a 3d seat and 3d on a shilling seat was not introduced until the wartime budget of 1916, so it was possible to charge only 1d, 2d and 3d for seats at the children's matinees, the adults accompanying children only being charged half the normal price.

For the 1911 Christmas show a group of local girls, wearing fetching Eskimo costumes, were to sing and dance between the two films. To dress for their parts they climbed up the narrow stairs to the newly acquired room next to the theatre which opened on to Dealing Yard.

The twelve, thirteen and fourteen year olds were highly excited- many foregoing their tea to be in time to savour to the full the atmosphere of the crowded, candle-lit dressing room.

Laughing and talking one child swung her white cotton-wool clad arm into a candle flame and in an instant the whole Eskimo costume was alight. In panic she screamed and ran to the narrow door brushing her flaming clothes against the other jostling children. Laughter turned to screams as the children fought their way to the door at the head of the steep steps, the draught making the flames all the more intense.

In the theatre no was aware of the disaster until the agonising screams of the children were heard coming from the yard. The possible panic there was avoided by the quick thinking and control of the manager, Abraham Taylor, who quietly emptied the auditorium.

In the yard parents, who had been waiting to see their children perform, were dowsing the flames with their bare hands. The pitifully injured youngsters were taken the short journey to the Royal Hospital where staff had been enjoying their own Christmas treat.

During the long night parents comforted their children as the medical staff did what they could to ease the frightful pain of burns that had made some of them unrecognisable. Despite their plea 'not to let them die' by the morning five little girls, Lydia Smith, Ada Tiddall, Mabel Swain, Winifred Wood, and Lizzie Bell were dead.

This 'unspeakable horror' temporarily closed the theatre which was improved in the spring of 1914 when it was reopened as The Cinema House, no longer combining films and live entertainment.

The weekly advertisements, whilst showing twice nightly performances at 7pm and 9pm now also named the performance, showing for the grand opening The Golden Beetle, a five-reeler being 'an Indian Jungle Romance'. Changes were made in the show twice a week, the Christmas films being The Grey Horror (three reels) at the beginning of the week with Oh my aunt! as the second feature and The Price of a Kiss (three exclusive reels) followed by The Broken Chain (episode one)-'the greatest serial yet screened', from Thursday to Saturday. And all this still for only 2d, 4d,6d and 9d with half price at matinees.

The cinema continued into the twenties but was never as popular after the fire as it had been before. Inevitably rumours were associated with the tragedy, one being that the pleading screams of the ill-fated girls could still be heard by cinema goers as they made their way home past The Yard late at night.

Charles Paxton Markham

The last of Chesterfield's flamboyant industrialists

WHEN JOSEPH PAXTON stole into the kitchen of Chatsworth in the morning of his joining the staff as the Head Gardener at Chatsworth he started an interesting chain of events that had a significant effect on the lives of many of the people of Chesterfield. For it was in the Chatsworth kitchen that he saw the girl whom he was to woo and marry. Paxton became not only the servant but also the friend and confidant of the Duke of Devonshire demonstrating his engineering skills in designing the Emperor fountain, the greenhouses and his crowning glory, the Crystal Palace, home of the Great Exhibition of 1851.

His daughter Rosa in her turn was wooed by, and married the Chesterfield industrialist Charles Markham. Charles Markham had commenced his career as a railway engineer but was recruited by the group of Manchester entrepreneurs, headed by Henry Davis Pochin who had recently purchased the Staveley coal and iron company from Richard Barrow, to take over the active management and re-vitalisation of the enterprise.

Under his direction, over the following quarter century, the output of coal and iron doubled, despite the challenge of the new cheap Bessemer steel, for Charles was a man of single purpose who trucked no interference with his ambition to build up the strength of the company. In this expansive age, when organised labour was starting to flex its muscles, clashes were inevitable and were made more bitter by Markham's deep-rooted objection to trade unions.

49

Charles Paxton Markham and
daughter, Violet, at Tapton House

He saw the future of the company as a dynastic heritage and groomed his eldest son Charles Paxton Markham as his heir. CP, as he became known, had the same industrial flair as his father but was of a much more relaxed temperament and recognised that human relations were changing and so was much more co-operative with the trade unions.

CP had been born at Brimington Hall, on the edge of Chesterfield, in April 1865 and grew up there with his two younger brothers and his sisters. The children were always included in the family circle and at Brimington, and later at Tapton House, they heard constant discussions about trade and markets and met many of the rich and famous. But there would have been little discussion about the conditions of the workers in the iron works or the collieries.

Straight from school CP joined his father at the Staveley iron works to be trained as his successor. He was a popular figure on the plant his bulldogish, dark good looks, giving him an honest air. And his ability was readily recognised, the elderly Board being very ready, when he reached his majority, to note in their minutes their appreciation of the activity and intelligence he had brought to bear on the company's business.

Two years later on his father's death he was appointed to fill the vacancy as a director of the company. For these first few years there was no permanent chairman but when Davis Pochin died CP started to take the chair at the annual general meetings and became permanent chairman in 1903, remaining in the post and actively leading the company for the next twenty three years.

He was never short of money, having inherited a sizeable fortune from his father, and enjoyed a slightly flamboyant life style preferring to be driven in a glorious primrose-yellow Rolls Royce than anything more mundane. His wealth was compounded by his childless, and often stormy marriage to Margaret 'Daisy' Jackson the daughter of the chairman of the rival Clay Cross Company. She was a remarkably handsome woman and played the role of 'lady bountiful' with considerable style enjoying their cruises in their private yacht in the Mediterranean and Scandinavia and entertaining at their grouse moor in Scotland.

She encouraged CP to involve himself in local politics and he served three terms as mayor of the Borough and as chairman of the justices' bench, his dry wit bringing enlivenment to what at times were very tedious proceedings. But he had no ambitions to involve himself in national politics though he gave some desultory support to his brother Arthur who was the Liberal M.P. for Mansfield from the turn of the century to his sudden death in 1916 (which so devastated their sister Violet).

All along he seemed to have the Midas touch enjoying outstanding success in his public and business careers.

On the death of his father, CP, still only aged twenty three, bought up the ailing Broad Oaks Works at Spital, on the banks of the River Rother, and re-directed its production to meet the burgeoning market for all the heavy equipment of the pre-First World War industrial age: rolling mills, colliery winding gear and blast furnaces. So dynamic was his management that within twenty years the work force was quadrupled to 600 and the products of the company led to his boast that a fifth of all the coal wound in Britain used equipment manufactured in Chesterfield.

At Staveley the production of pig iron rose with similar certainty, more than doubling in the thirteen years before the First World War. The supply of locally mined iron-stone petered out by

Queen Victoria's Golden Jubilee and more and more was brought in from Northampton, Rutland and Lincoln. CP joined the Staveley company in enterprises with other iron producers, John Brown of Sheffield, Sheepbridge and Bestwood Coal and Iron to exploit these ore fields, his Markham company often winning the contracts to build the quarry traction locomotives and all the other paraphernalia of iron-stone quarrying.

CP's long view was demonstrated in the Edwardian period when the prospects for iron production looked poor. He successfully negotiated a further ninety year lease for a works site from the Duke of Devonshire and persuaded the Staveley board to build three new blast furnaces with an associated coke plant. Markham acted as the engineer and working virtually night and day completed the project in two years. His new ovens could process local soft coal, previously unusable in this way and gave rise to the important chemical branch of the company's activities. By 1921 further additions had made the works, according to a technical trade journal, 'one of the finest modern ironworks in the kingdom'.

The funding of these new works owed much to CP's financing skills and his ability to persuade the banks to lend and to raise debentures and, by his death, the company and its subsidiaries employed over 37,000 people; less than a tenth in the Devonshire iron and chemical works, the majority being in the associated company collieries.

Building up the company had not been without its traumas and Charles Paxton was not always the most popular figure in Chesterfield. But he always respected his working force trying to alleviate the impact of strikes on the families of his men by providing free meals for striking colliers' children, improving housing at Hollingwood and openly recognising that masters did not do enough for their work people.

During his lifetime he funded the building of the Staveley working men's club and a rest home at Holymoorside and at his death in 1926 gave the borough his home at Tapton.

Paxton's Rosa would surely have been proud of all that her son did for Chesterfield.

A Most Superior Person

The story of Lord Curzon of Kedleston

LADY SCARSDALE APPEARED TO HAVE psychic powers. On one occasion she recounted how, late one evening, while she and her husband, the Second Viscount Scarsdale were sitting in their room at Kedleston she suddenly shivered and felt decidedly uncomfortable. She told Lord Scarsdale that 'Uncle George was saying that he was feeling terribly cold'. She persisted that something should be done and finally a reluctant Lord Scarsdale agreed. Late though it was, he went down to the crypt, for Uncle George had been dead for fifty years. When the door was opened it was found a water main had broken and the crypt was half full of water.

Uncle George, born in 1859, was that 'most superior person' George Nathaniel Curzon, eldest son of the 4th Lord Scarsdale whose established lineage was traced, unbroken, to the Norman Conquest, although his Irish peerage dated only from 1761. Much neglected by his parson father and as much so by his mother he grew up in a fairly loveless Kedleston spending a fair amount of time in the servants' hall and being disciplined by a merciless governess.

But his intellectual brilliance shone through and though, as his letters home show, he was very lonely at Eton, envying the visitors other boys had, he collected all the major school prizes before going on to Balliol college, Oxford. There he was an outstanding scholar, renowned for his wit as much as his academic brilliance. It was as an undergraduate, in reply to Oscar Wilde, that he wrote the lines 'My name is George Nathaniel Curzon / I am a most Superior Person', an epithet that was long to remain with him. And, although he won an immediate fellowship to the graduate college of All Souls he suffered a smarting blow to his pride by only being awarded a second class degree in Greats (Classic History and Philosophy). So damaged was his pride that he said he would devote the rest of his life to showing that the examiners had made a mistake. And this he indeed did becoming Chancellor of the University in 1907.

As a young man he travelled widely, much of the way on horseback (that gave him great back pain) in the Near East, taking in Egypt and going on to Russia, Persia, Afghanistan, India, Burma and even making a short visit to Japan. By the time he was thirty he had twice been around the world, supporting himself by selling articles to the *Times* and publishing books about his journeys that were renowned for their prose style and wit. The epitome of a conservative he said he would never think of travelling without a dress suit.

Aged 26, later than many had expected, he made his entry into politics being elected as the M.P. for Southport. Recognition and promotion came rapidly and within five years he was Under Secretary for India then Under Secretary for Foreign Affairs before being appointed Viceroy and Governor General of India in 1898.

In his early years Curzon had been relatively short of money but his money worries had been completely put behind him in 1885 when he married the beautiful Mary Victoria Leiter,the daughter of an American millionaire who promptly settled a million dollars on his daughter and established substantial annual incomes for bride and groom.

Royal support was also forthcoming, Queen Victoria feeling that it was appropriate that she was represented by a peer in India. But she recognised that he might wish to return, at a later date, to the House of Commons, and so left that door open by creating him as the First Baron Curzon of Kedleston in the Irish peerage.

His impact on the administration of India was again outstanding. The reforms to the currency and administration he introduced (although he was a bit of an 'in triplicate' bureaucrat himself) were of lasting benefit to the sub-continent. The reorganisation he made of the government of Bengal was not well received by the Hindu population but his wit, dignity and panache coupled with a flare for pomp, elevated the standing of Viceregal house. It was crowned by the magnificent spectacle of the Durbar of 1903 when Lady Curzon wore her peacock gown that was festooned with a rajah's ransom of precious stones. He always had an interest

in fine and historic buildings and it is to him that we owe the sympathetic restoration of the Taj Mahal (and nearer home Tattersall and Bodian Castles).

At the same time Lord Kitchener was Commander-in-Chief of the army in India. Equally larger than life, despite the size of the country, there was not room for them both and so serious a quarrel developed between Curzon and Kitchener about how the army should be run that Curzon resigned, after seven years as Viceroy, and returned home. Both he and his wife had suffered from the climate of India and Lady Curzon died in the following year leaving an unfilled gap in Curzon's private and public life until his much later second marriage to Grace, the widow of the American author Alfred Duggan.

Provision had been made for him to re-enter the Commons but he elected instead to enter the Lords as a representative of the Irish peers. It was a decision he was probably to regret later.

After six years of service in the Lords he was created an Earl in 1911 and was drawn into Lloyd George's war cabinet as Lord Privy Seal becoming Foreign Secretary after the Armistice. More honours followed, the Garter, and elevation to be Marquess Curzon of Kedleston in 1921, the year after one of his three daughters, Cynthia, married the up and coming Oswald Mosley.

When Bonar-Law, the Prime Minister, stood down in 1924 it was widely expected that Curzon would take up the reins of office. But George V was advised otherwise, the prospect of having the leader of the Government in the Lords being considered no longer acceptable, Baldwin instead being asked to form an Administration. Curzon was devastated. Always a highly strung and emotional man he was reduced to tears and never recovered from this last unexpected blow to his pride. The family motto 'Let Curzon hold what Curzon held' remained true. It did not embrace what had not been held however close it came to being within grasp.

Within the year he died and, after a funeral service at Westminster Abbey, his remains were brought back to be interred in the chilly crypt at his home, Kedleston.

Erasmus Darwin

The Epitome of the Polymath

CHESTERFIELD SCHOOL, in the mid-seventeen hundreds, had the reputation of being amongst the foremost academic institutions in northern England. It was not, then, surprising that William Darwin, the lord of the manor of Elston, some five miles south of Newark, should have elected to send his second son Erasmus, when he was ten, to join his brother at Chesterfield School.

Erasmus had been born into a boisterous family in the winter of 1731. The boys liked playing practical jokes and Erasmus only narrowly escaped drowning when he fell in, having been made by his brothers to walk along a precipitous river edge with a sack pulled down closely over his head and body. On another occasion he received such a blow to his head that it left him permanently with a white shock of hair.

He was an exemplary pupil benefiting from the tuition of the headmaster William Burrow and letters written at this time to his sister show a real talent in the handling of words.

He moved on when he was eighteen to St John's College, Cambridge where he was awarded the Exeter scholarship, of sufficient value to relieve the financial burden the boys made on their father. His brother Robert was attracted to poetry which was published early in his career and Erasmus showed the same flair, having a poem, on the theme of the death of Frederick Prince of Wales, published.

While he toyed with the possibility of earning a living as a poet he was encouraged by his father to pursue a career in medicine. This took him to Edinburgh University until he returned to

Cambridge to take his M.B. degree in 1755.

Full of enthusiasm he set up his plate in Nottingham and suffered the indignity of not attracting any patients. The setback was fortunately only temporary for, when he transferred his location to Lichfield, he quickly built up a thriving practice (his income rising to £1065; 7: 6d by 1771), and soon established a reputation as a doctor over a wide area. This reputation continued to grow, his patients including Josiah Wedgewood, whose knees had been seriously impaired by childhood smallpox and many more famous people. His reputation was so enhanced that King George III said many times 'Why does Dr Darwin not come to London? He shall be my physician if he comes.'

But he was not a narrow-minded physician. His interests ranged over the wide sphere of the new sciences that were interesting gentlemen at this time. He encouraged the experiments of Boulton and Watt, collected methane from his garden pond to help the experiments of Joseph Priestley and was a designer and inventor of stature, although no single invention is associated with his name. To stimulate the interchange of ideas he founded the Lunar Society of which Priestley was a member and Wedgwood, Herschel and Joseph Banks were guests.

His practical approach led to his design of a horizontal windmill with a vertical axis, and following the analysis of phonetical sounds he made a working speaking machine using a primitive bellows. The accident he sustained when his carriage overturned led to a new design for coach springs, S-shaped wheel spoke and modifications to the towing pole.

Throughout his life his interest in writing poetry continued, and though he spoke with a stammer and the loss of his front teeth further impaired his speech, he was a good speaker and reader of his own poetry. Much of this, and his prose, deals with philosophical ideas but he was always moved to write about the people and things he saw about him in this age of industrial expansion.

Of Brindley, who designed the Chesterfield canal, he wrote;

'So with the strong arm immortal Brindley leads
His long canals, and parts the velvet meads:
Winding his lucid lines, the watery mass
Mines the firm rock, or loads the deep morass.'

His polymath interests included botany and he laboriously translated many thousand of pages of the Swedish scientist Linnaeus' text on the classification of plants. His own work on evolution, in some ways, contains more adventurous ideas than those of his much more famous grand-son Charles Darwin.

Charles's father, Robert, like his brothers, found their father imperious and irascible, (though he displayed considerable benevolence in dealing with his poorer patients) but he was interested in the progress of their careers.

Erasmus had married Mary Howard soon after moving to Lichfield and she had borne him a daughter as well as the four boys. Throughout her motherhood she suffered great pain and sought relief in drinking spirits. These destroyed her liver and it was this experience that led the Doctor to adopt a life of abstinence.

Following his wife's death in 1770, when she was only 30, a certain Miss Seward hoped she might be his second wife. It was not to be, Darwin instead seeking comfort in the close company of Miss Parker of Ashbourne, a town he frequently visited. They had two daughters, Susan and Mary, whom Erasmus openly acknowledged as his own. When they were growing up he wrote an interesting 'directive' on the education of young women and later financed the opening of their teaching establishment in Ashbourne.

But his appetite for ladies was not sated there and in 1781 Erasmus married the widow of Col Chandos-Pole who already had four children and who was to bear Darwin a second family of seven children, four of them boys.

To accommodate his extending family he moved to Breadsall Priory and there after what was probably a heart attack he died suddenly and peacefully in the late evening of April, 18th, 1802.

Fortunately a number of paintings of the rather clumsy, shambling man, with his head shrunk into his chest have survived and we can visualise him talking to Dr Johnson, whom he didn't much like. And, although he is perhaps too readily referred to as Charles Darwin's grandfather, we can endorse the view of Headmaster William Burrow that in Erasmus we have a most distinguished old boy of Chesterfield School.

A Thread through the Renaissance

The story of Thomas Linacre, academic, churchman and physician to Henry VIII

L ONG BEFORE THE LAND around Old Brampton blazed yellow with the flowers of rape, grown for the oil from its seed, the open fields were blue with the flowers of flax. Flax was also grown to produce oil, linseed, but more importantly to make into linen. So common was the crop long ago that it gave its name to the area- Linacre.

Today the old fields lie mainly under the three reservoirs built early in the century to supply water to the borough of Chesterfield. No longer needed for that purpose the valley is being converted to a nature reserve and leisure park.

Close to the middle reservoir there once stood a sizeable mansion, Linacre Hall, the home of the Linacre family, who as was common in the middle ages, took their name from the place where they lived. All visible traces of the house have disappeared, but occasionally when the Severn Trent Water company are doing repair work they come across what must be remains of the old buildings.

The most famous member of the family was Thomas Linacre, born in 1460. Little is known about his boyhood but he must have been a bright boy who enjoyed his years at school and university.

After graduating at Oxford at the age of 18 he was elected to a Fellowship of All Souls College and began to make an impact on the "establishment". Latin was the language of scholars at this time and probably none were familiar with Greek.

Linacre College, Oxford

It was to learn Greek that Thomas set off to the universities of Italy: Florence, Rome and Padua. He was soon extremely proficient in the language and went on to study medicine graduating at Padua as a Doctor of Medicine in 1496.

It was in Italy that he met such influential men as Lorenzo di Medici and the printer Aldus Manutius of Venice. His stay of 12 years in Italy was rounded off by a short return to Venice where he helped Manutius in his first translated publication of Aristotle.

On his return to Oxford he continued his studies, graduating again as M.D. At the same time he started teaching Greek at the university, a practice in England that had died out with the passing of the Venerable Bede. Amongst his pupils were Thomas More and Erasmus.

The elegance of his translations into Latin from Greek of the medical works of Galen (who died in 200 A.D.) added to Thomas' fame. His profound scholarship brought him to the attention of King Henry VII who recruited him as a tutor and physician to his eldest son Arthur, who was already ailing. Later in life, after Arthur's death,

Thomas Linacre

he was appointed in 1509 as physician to Henry VIII and later, after writing an impossibly difficult Latin grammar, as a tutor of Latin to Henry's daughter Mary, the Queen for five years from 1553. As physician to the King he was called on to treat Cardinal Wolsey.

The King rewarded him with appointments to various ecclesiastical posts from which he drew the revenues, paying deputies to perform the religious ceremonials for he was not himself ordained until he was 60 years old.

Although he held high offices in the church his first loves were scholarship and medicine and he continued to combine his royal duties with teaching at Oxford.

It was Linacre who took the earliest steps to put medicine on a scientific basis, being at pains to stamp out quackery. And it was through his efforts that the College of Physicians was founded in 1518 and chartered in 1523, with Thomas as the first president.

He died in 1524 and was buried, as he had wished, in St.Paul's Cathedral. By one of his two wills he left property and books to both Merton College, Oxford and St.John's, Cambridge for the establishment of Linacre Lectureships to promote the study of medicine.

On a cold winter's day, nearly five hundred years after his birth, Thomas Linacre was honoured in his home parish by the anonymous provision, by a prominent Chesterfield family, of new oak stalls and clergy desks in the parish church of Saint Peter and St. Paul. Pageantry and a splash of colour was added by the attendance of many medical men and scholars in academic dress. The plaque attached to the stalls records the highlights of his life and deservedly attributes to Dr Thomas Linacre a principal role in the revival of classical learning in this country. Some say that when he came back from Italy he brought with him the first Damask roses. These still bloom in old-fashioned gardens andperhaps blue flax will one day bloom once more around Linacre.

New light on the Lady of the Lamp

An account of the many little-known talents of Florence Nightingale

THE NAME FLORENCE NIGHTINGALE immediately conjures up the long open wards at Scutari during the Crimea war and the healing light shed from the lamp held aloft by the indomitable Florence ministering to the needs of the sick and dying soldiers. But very little is usually known about her as a mathematician, statistician, administrator and manipulator of government departments.

Florence, named after the city of her birth, was born into a well-connected upper-class family, the daughter of William and Frances Nightingale. Her father, surprisingly for a Victorian, believed in the education of girls (especially his own) and Florence and her sister were fortunate to learn not only the classics, Greek, Latin and Italian but also history and mathematics. Given a considerable grounding in mathmatics by her father and aunt the young Florence was also taught by James Sylvester an internationally eminent mathematician

In 1837, when she was just seventeen she experienced, at Embley Park, what she thought of as her first Christian divine calling, to devote her life to the care of others especially through nursing. This commitment was not approved of by her parents but she got her own way, visited Germany and aged twenty five began her nursing career.

The story of how she was asked to recruit nurses to deal with the appalling conditions in the Crimea military hospitals, revealed by

the Times newspaper, and how in 1854 she and a staff of 38 women were sent by Sidney Herbert to Turkey and browbeat the military establishment to establish her nursing regime has been told many times but less has been said about the extremely valuable work she did in collecting data and systematising record-keeping practices. It was her interpretation of this data which made possible the calculation of mortality rates that showed how improved sanitation would result in fewer deaths; this at a time when deaths from disease and neglect were greater than through enemy action.

On her return to England her statistical work attracted the

attention of Dr. William Farr, the Complier of Abstracts in the General Registry Office, who as an epidemiologist was pre-eminent in compiling the data that found the cause of the outbreaks of cholera that plagued Victorian London. With his guidance she studied statistical methods and came to the alarming conclusion that he was right and that disease came from a contaminated environment and that she might have been responsible in some ways for the deaths of soldiers at Scutari

Farr and Nightingale jointly realised that the world could be improved by better sanitation and that the government would only be convinced of this by the provision of hard evidence based on meticulously kept records. Their efforts were rewarded by the setting up in 1857 of a Royal Commission into sanitary conditions to look into the health of the army with Sydney Herbert as chairman. As a woman Florence could not be appointed to the Royal Commission but she wrote the report of over a thousand pages including the detailed statistical reports and was instrumental in the implementation of its recommendations.

Her most original contribution to the work had been her invention of polar-area charts where the statistic being presented is shown in proportion to the area of a wedge in a circular diagram similar to a modern pie diagram but with area extended by proportionally extended radii, or a circular histogram. Its use of colours to distinguish deaths caused by preventable diseases such as cholera and dysentery, deaths from wounds and from all other causes led to it being known as the Nightingale rose or a 'coxcomb' as she called it Incomprehensible written material suddenly became pictorially understandable. With it, as her sanitary reforms were introduced, she was able to demonstrate how deaths had fallen. Its use in her published works, it was said, at least encouraged Queen Victoria to look at the pictures!

She felt that the official report lacked bite and in 1858 she privately printed and distributed her 'unpublished evidence of the public health disaster at Scutari'.

The preparation and subsequent work on the Royal Commission affected her health, already damaged by the Crimea fever that had brought her home from Scutari and she suffered what today we would know as chronic fatigue syndrome. With it a new phase of her life began in the role of an invalid though not before the Nightingale Trust Fund had been set up with Sydney Herbert as the honorary secretary and the Duke of Cumberland as chairman and the Nightingale Training school had been established at St Thomas's hospital London. And she had published her slim volume Notes on Nursing in 1860. A number of other works were to follow.

In this new role, while still promoting female nursing and improved nursing practice and advocating military and public hygiene, she concentrated more on influencing government continuing to be helped by Sydney Herbert who was no longer a minister. In 1858 she was appointed as the first female fellow of the Royal Statistical Society of London. Further major contributions came in the development of a Model Statistical Form to allow hospitals to collect and produce consistent data and statistical information. American statisticians recognised her contribution to their work by appointing her, in 1874, an honorary member of the American Statistical Association and Karl Pearson, the father of mathematical statistics, acknowledged her as the 'prophetess' in the development of applied statistics.

Some would say that in these years Florence was, apart from the Queen, the best known person in Britain. She was awarded the Royal Red Cross by Victoria in 1883 and in 1907 became the first woman to be awarded the Order of Merit. She died in 1910 aged 90.

Mary Seacole may now steal some of Florence Nightingale's Crimean thunder but her mathematical works alone set her apart and it is indeed fortunate that in her own words, 'God spoke to me and called me to His service.'

The Foljambes of Chesterfield

W HEN, IN 1249, Sir John Foljambe was near to death, he expressed a desire to be buried in the church at Tideswell alongside his forefathers. For it was here, in Tideswell, that the senior branch of the family had held land as crown servants and exercised sway since the Norman Conquest. His descendant John Foljambe, who died 109 years later, is commemorated by an impressive brass commissioned in 1875 to replace the brass lost from the matrix in the chancel of the Cathedral of the Peak. The knightly figure, clothed in armour with a sword by his side, wears the Foljambe tabard emblazoned with a bend and six escallops. At his head is a ribbon bearing the inscription 'Look, now I sleep in dust, but I know that my Redeemer lives'.

A similar tranquillity prevails in the Lady or Foljambe chapel in the Spire church of Chesterfield. Here lie the remains of the junior branch of the family that had acquired the manor of Walton in the time of Richard II through the marriage of Thomas Foljambe to the heiress of Loudham and Breton, the former lords of the manor.

But the tranquillity surrounding the tombs of the sixteenth century Foljambes does not reflect the turbulence of their ancestors during the troublesome times of the Wars of the Roses and Henry V's and the infant Henry VI's sorties into re-establishing a claim to the largely lost old Norman French empire.

These were times of considerable political and economic upheaval and the local gentry families exploited the unrest to increase their own power or make an insecure future more secure.

Near Chesterfield the overwhelmingly powerful families were the Foljambes of Chesterfield, the Leekes of Sutton and the

Sir Godfrey and his wife are buried in an ostentatious tomb situated in the Lady Chapel of St. Mary and All Saints Church, Chesterfield

Pierponts of Holme, in Nottingham. And they lost no opportunity of bettering one another.

The force of such feuding is illustrated by the attack made on New Year's day, 1422, by a group of two hundred Lancastrian supporters led by Thomas Foljambe of Walton, Richard Foljambe of Bonsall and Thomas Cokke of Bakewell on the unsuspecting congregation at mass in the parish church. Thomas Mogyton, the parish clerk, who was in league with the assailants, had locked the doors to the belfry, vestry and crucifix chamber before tolling the bell to summon those coming from Bakewell in support of Thomas Foljambe.

They burst in, armed with battle axes and with swords drawn, and stood at the west end close to the font. Courageously the vicar confronted them carrying the eucharist and warned them of the dire consequences of carrying on with their plans. But their blood was up and pleading was no avail. Three burgesses standing at the chancel had their thumbs severed and then two of them, Henry Longford and William Bradshaw, were killed. The third, Henry Pierpont, was led outside and though the mob bayed for his death the intervention of Richard Foljambe saved his life and he was sent home maimed and bleeding.

There was almost a repeat performance twelve years later when the Foljambes, who had been strengthening their position in Scarsdale, were involved in a most unseemly but violent battle in the Chesterfield parish churchyard.

For the outrage of 1422 Thomas Foljambe was declared a murderer but it was not until thirty two years later that he and ninety of the assaulting mob that still survived, many coming from Chesterfield were cast into the Marshalsea prison to await trial. Unfortunately, the outcome of the trial has not come down to us.

Throughout these turbulent times the Foljambes continued to acquire property in Chesterfield the heir Henry, in the late fifteenth century, buying up single properties or small estates extending his holdings in Newbold and Normanton, until by 1498 he was able to claim to be a burgess of Chesterfield holding lands there next in size only to King Henry VII's.

The next Tudor monarch favoured Henry's heir Godfrey who fought with the king in France and as a reward was given a life grant of the stewardship of the hundred of Scarsdale and the manor of Chesterfield, an office he retained even though the hundred and manor passed to the Talbots in 1531. Godfrey continued with the acquisition of land bringing Boythorpe into the family holding and being able, on his death in 1541, to hand considerable control over the affairs of Chesterfield to his eldest son Sir James.

But already the seeds of decline were being sown. Sir James was succeeded by another Sir Godfrey during whose lifetime the sale of part of the estate holdings was commenced. And it is from his death in 1595 that the influence of the family in Chesterfield steadily declined.

In Chesterfield he is best remembered for the three charities created by his will: one setting up a trust to finance a lectureship at the parish church, the second providing funds to relieve the suffering of the poor and the third to found a grammar school with a master to be paid £13 6s 8d a year.

With the decline of local influence went the demise of the family seat at Walton. The great house standing in its large park was demolished as was the nearby family chapel, the remains of which had survived until 1810, and which had acknowledged its subservience to the mother Church at Chesterfield.　　　All that now survives to commemorate the once powerful family is the street name and the ostentatious tombs. The name Foljambe means 'false leg' and perhaps, as in the Eyre family, some knightly member early on had lost a leg in battle. The significance of that missing limb is punned in the corner of one of the altar tombs, in the church of St Mary's and All Saints, commemorating Sir Godfrey and his spouse Isabel buried like that early Sir John, 'where their forefathers had been buried before'.

The Keyes of Staveley

unlock some of the secrets of the Gunpowder Plot

W HEN GOOD QUEEN BESS graciously granted a charter to the burgesses of Chesterfield in 1598 they were delighted, enjoying as they were peace and prosperity. But her Roman Catholic subjects were not so elated persecuted as they were by a series of pernicious statutes. These draconian laws barred Catholics from holding office, practising at the bar or attending the universities. Priests found guilty of saying the Mass were deemed to have committed treason and could be sentenced to a vile death, and even those Catholics failing to attend church services each Sunday and Feast day could be fined a shilling (almost a week's wages) for failing to attend. Nor were woman spared, Margaret Clitheroe of York being squeezed to death under eight hundredweight of rocks piled on her body because she would not plead when charged with concealing a priest.

It is not then surprising that Catholics welcomed the accession, in 1603, of James I who was known to be sympathetic to their cause, and whose wife, the Danish princess, Anne, had converted to Catholicism. Rumours abounded about the intention to repeal the repressive Act of Supremacy and initiate an age of toleration. But such hopes were short lived and the Jesuit priests and the Catholic community soon realised that intolerance was to continue as the order of the day.

It was this realisation that soured Robert Keyes of Staveley and made him a willing convert to the scheme of the charming and handsome Robert Catesby: "the scheme that's never been forgot".

Robert Keyes, a tall, red-bearded yeoman, was born around 1565, probably in Staveley where his father Edward Keyes was the rector of the church of Saint John the Baptist. The family were near relatives of the Frechevilles, (Lords of the Manor of Staveley), Peter Frecheville, who died in 1582, having married Margaret, the widow of Francis Woodrove and the daughter of Arthur Key (or Kay) of Almonbury, Yorkshire. Edward Keye, a protestant priest, had been appointed rector in 1547 and continued in the benefice to around 1607 when Edward Birkbeck (who later married Anne, Edward's widow) was appointed rector. Anne was the daughter of Sir Robert Tyrrwhitt a committed Catholic from Lincolnshire and it was her religious beliefs that her son Robert adopted despite his father's rectorship.

His Catholic leanings were endorsed by his wife Christiana who was a widow with children when Robert married her. She was a clever woman and acted as governess to the children of Lord Mordaunt, a Roman Catholic peer living in Northampton, (who was to suffer a swingeing fine later from this connection). A further

Catholic link for Robert was his cousin, the beautiful Elizabeth Tyrrwhitt who was married to the recusant Ambrose Rookwood of Coldham Hall, Suffolk, who in his turn fell in with Catesby.

Robert Catesby was a charismatic man, over six feet tall and handsome with a capability of charming the birds out of the trees. It was he who master-minded the conspiracy to lease the ground floor of a small house situated under the chamber used as the House of Lords, fill it with gunpowder and by blowing up the opening of Parliament cause such a commotion that in the confusion James' daughter, the young Princess Elizabeth, could be declared Queen. She was to be cultivated in the adoption of the religion that would return England to the glorious Catholic traditions of Queen Mary Tudor.

To execute his plan Catesby recruited Tom Wintour, Jack Wright, Thomas Percy, (Wright's brother-in-law) and Guido Fawkes. They met together at the Duck and Drake Inn, in London and agreed that Percy would arrange the lease and Fawkes, who was an experienced officer having served with the Spanish forces in Flanders, would ferry the powder across the river and be responsible for setting the fuse trail and lighting the charge. But first the gunpowder had to be assembled and temporarily stored and it was with this in view that Robert Keyes and Thomas Bates, a sort of up-market servant, in October 1604, were made privy to the conspiracy. Keyes in particular was to keep an eye on Catesby's London house where the powder was stored. Obtaining powder was relatively easy and without being made privy to the secret Ambrose Rookwood was asked to obtain powder, ostensibly to send to troops in Flanders.

Parliament had been adjourned in July 1604 and was due to reassemble in February, 1605. It was then that the deed was to be done. But such well laid plans of mice and men were soon awry.

An outbreak of plague led to a further postponement of Parliament to mid-summer and plans were developed to kidnap the young princess after the destruction of the king and his heir, the boy prince, Henry. More hands were needed to muster horses and co-ordinate activities throughout the Midlands where the Princess was living. And with the belief that there would be Spanish support to an insurrection heavy war-horses would need to be assembled.

More conspirators were recruited, including Keyes' cousin-in-law, Ambrose Rookwood, Robert Wintour, John Grant and Kit Wright to be joined later by Francis Tresham, and the dashing 24 year old Sir Everard Digby.

Much soul searching went on amongst the plotters for it was clear that the explosion would not only kill the King, a legitimate target in their view, but also many Catholic Lords and, most despicably, the young children of the King. All seemed agreed that the ends justified the means.

Then plague rolled round the city again and men feared to come to Whitehall. Parliament was again postponed to November.

As the final days approached tension ran high. At the last moment Lord Monteagle received a mysterious anonymous note warning him not to attend the opening ceremony. He took it to Lord Salisbury who appeared to prevaricate and then had the houses around Westminster searched by Sir Thomas Knevett. The barrels of powder were discovered and Guido Fawkes, under his alias John Johnson, 'servant of Thomas Percy' was found and arrested. The game was up.

Within days the thirteen conspirators were uncovered, some in London and others in the Midlands. In the shoot-out of the capture Robin Catesby and Thomas Percy died. Their hastily buried bodies were latter exhumed and their par-boiled severed heads were sent to London.

Those brought to London were subjected to torture in the Tower, with Francis Tresham dying of a lung infection just before Christmas. Torture had been abolished in England in the middle ages and had only been re-introduced by Henry VIII, (probably taking his lead from the Spanish Inquisition). Now on the express instructions James, Fawkes, a strong young man, aged 34 and with an iron will, was relentlessly tortured by the hanging manacles and then on the only rack in the country housed at the Tower. Keyes and the others suffered similar fates.

Their 'confessions' were made much of at their show trial for High Treason staged in the last freezing days of January, 1606, at Westminster Hall and watched from a screened room by the King and Prince Henry. Keyes said little at the trial but showed no shortage of courage preferring to die rather than live in the midst of what he saw as such tyranny. The outcome was a foregone conclusion and execution was fixed for Thursday, 30th January and Friday, the 31st.

Four were executed where Queen Elizabeth had made her famous speech on the defeat of the Armada and on Friday Tom Wintour, Ambrose Rookwood, Guy Fawkes and Robert Keyes were brought from the Tower to Westminster, the site of their intended crime. All the conspirators were dragged on woven hurdles tied to horses' tails, their faces close to the ground so as not to contaminate the air, through streets lined with spectators.

The scaffold platform was raised so that the populace could view the scene and the prisoners were required to climb a short ladder to where the hangman placed his noose. The last to be executed, Fawkes, was so broken in body that he had to be half-dragged up the steps, but Keyes who went before him attempted to defy the horror of the final processes by jumping from the ladder hoping to break his neck. His luck deserted him and the rope broke. Alive, he was taken to the adjacent bench where he was emasculated, his chest and abdomen were torn open and his heart held up with the executioner's cry 'Here is the heart of a traitor'. The head joined the others on stakes and the separated limbs were left out as carrion. Not one abjured their faith and all died Catholics.

The subsequent torture and trials of Jesuit priests never adduced any evidence that the whole conspiracy was more than a fanatical terrorists' ill thought-out escapade but the enormity of the potential crime slipped easily into mythology and coincided nicely with the pagan ceremonies of failing light at the onset of winter.

Unfortunately, there is no way of knowing what the Reverend Edward Keyes thought of his son's small part in the national crime. Did it perhaps hasten his death in 1607?

The Wealthiest Commoner in England

the rise and rise of Sir Gilbert Heathcote

THE 1711 LORD MAYOR OF LONDON, dressed in a full bottomed wig and civic robes of handsome silk, looks down, with eye brows quizzically raised as if saying, 'I know you're from Chesterfield, but what do you want?' He was Sir Gilbert Heathcote and his painting hangs in the court-room of St. Thomas' hospital, London.

His great-grandfather, Thomas, was a successful butcher who farmed in Loads, Old Brampton and Chesterfield. As the local aristocracy played a smaller and smaller direct part in running local industry Thomas, and other tradesmen like him, put their surplus funds into financing the lead trade. It proved a sound investment and added to the already considerable Heathcote family fortune.

Thomas' one son, George, bought Cutthorpe Hall from the Foljambe family in 1614, when the Foljambes were finding it necessary to convert some of their assets into cash as their fortunes declined, and his daughter went on to marry well into the Rodes family of Barlborough and Staveley.

Another of his sons, Gilbert, was born with a silver spoon in his mouth being the god-child of the Earl of Shrewsbury. He amassed a fortune from his interests in lead mining and industry in Staveley

that brought in the incredible sum of £5,000 a year, until he lost a great portion of it by injudicious speculation.

This Gilbert lived in Souter Street, modern St. Mary's Gate, at the house, built at the end of the fifteenth century on the site of the abandoned house of the Dean of Lincoln, (now the Heathcote Restaurant).

He was an alderman of Chesterfield corporation but made the mistake of backing the Parliamentary cause and his refusal to take an oath of allegiance to Charles II cost him his seat on the council.

Married to Anne, the daughter of Thomas Dickens, he was blessed with a large family of whom seven sons survived, all being successful merchant-princes.

The eldest of them was born in 1650/1, the same year as Nell Gwyn and the year King Charles II landed in Scotland to be crowned king. He was named after his father and grew up in Chesterfield and, though there is no record he very likely went to the town's grammar school. His graduation at eighteen is recorded at Christ's College , Cambridge where he took his Master's degree in 1673.

Chesterfield was then still a backswood town with only a very inadequate access to the great world outside. The young Gilbert realised this and took himself off to live in St. Dunstan's-in-the-East, London, carrying on a wine importer's business with Spain, from premises in St. Swithin's Lane.

He had a natural flair for business which soon expanded to cover many other products beside wine and took in trading with Jamaica and the East Indies. It was in connection with his East Indian trading that he made history.

The East India Company had impounded the ship 'Redbridge', on a venture in which Gilbert Heathcote had a share, claiming that the company had a monopoly of the trade with India. Gilbert successfully challenged this, counter-claiming before Parliament that he had the right to trade where he would unless Parliament forbade it.

Heathcote then exploited this legal victory by promoting a new East India Company putting up no less than £10,000 of his own money as part of the capital. It prospered and by 1720 Gilbert was the Governor of the Company.

It was of such renown that the future Czar, Peter the Great, while he was in London, attended one of the company's directing board meetings where Gilbert was able to address him in what is described as 'high Dutch' to extol the virtue of tobacco smoking and to plead for its importation into the Czar's domains.

His financial flair led him to play a very active part in the formation of the Bank of England and he was elected to the first court at its inception in 1694. Twelve years later when the Bank's charter was extended he had made £60,0000 from the venture and took over as governor.

He was also elected to parliament, expelled for circulating exchequer bills, then re-elected only to charter a stormy passage in attempting to lighten the burden of the tithe acts.

Despite his enormous fortune, over £700,000 at his death, making him the richest commoner in England, he had a fearful reputation for parsimony complaining, for example, of the few shillings charged for the burial of his own brother. This led in his life time to his being mocked by the essayist, Pope, who thinly disguises his reference to the meanness of Heathcote.

He was particularly unpopular with the poor and in 1715 there was a plot to murder him and other magistrates by burning their houses. This came to nought but his coach was stopped as he was returning from the Commons where he was a member and all three of the occupants were robbed. He was so unpopular that when he had been elected Lord Mayor against considerable opposition, the mayoral procession had to be cancelled, Heathcote riding to the city on horseback and the livery companies attending by barges on the river.

But for all his unpopularity and reputation for meanness he was in many ways a considerable public benefactor giving a great deal of public service, for which he was knighted in 1702 and was created a baronet 30 years later. He not only served as a councillor but also as sheriff and was a colonel of the blue regiment of the trained bands, president of St. Thomas' hospital, master of the Vinters' Company and a commissioner for the colony of Georgia.

There is no record of his ever coming back to Chesterfield but he followed the example of his mother and brothers giving £400 to set up a charity to assist poor boys of the town in apprenticeships, or 'in putting out to trade or to sea'. He preferred to live in Rutland where he bought Normanton, the Mackworth family seat. It was here, in his eighty third year, that he died in January, 1733, ending a colourful and sometimes very stormy life.

The expression in his painting remains too awesome to venture an answer to his unspoken question.

Chesterfield's Early Sortie into the Iron Trade

O N A GREY AUTUMN DAY IN 1775, a pall of acrid smoke drifted slowly across from Wheatbridge to West Bars and set the asthmatic market toll-keeper coughing. It was more sulphurous than the smoke from the Brampton potteries and came from the stacks of coal at the newly opened Griffen foundry where John Smith was making coke for his furnaces.

Smith, with some Sheffield colleagues, had taken a lease of the foundry and iron-making furnace just outside the borough boundary together with the neighbouring forge and boring mill. They were cashing in on the burgeoning demand for iron for civil and ordnance use and the availability of cheap water transport when the canal to Stockwith opened in the following year.

The area around Chesterfield was blessed with coal and high quality dogs-tooth iron ore relatively close to the surface and easy to mine and a source of the iron-making flux, limestone, at Crich. Coal mines, first working as bell pits and later as long wall workings, were opening up around the town and Smith drew his coal locally from Boythorpe colliery and mines at Townend and Upperground, in Staveley. The ore he needed he won under license from the Duke of Devonshire at Calow.

The firm made a shaky start and really only got going under Ebenezer the second son of the founding John Smith. He was helped by the demand that was stimulated by the wars with the French, the

requirements of the bridge builders, the Newcomen steam engine makers, and those pioneers trying to use iron to make everything from church stoves and cupboard doors to building stanchions and tomb memorials.

But he was not the sole supplier from Chesterfield. The Hunlokes had operated an iron furnace at Wingerworth using charcoal in the smelt since the previous century but had been glad to sell it to Joseph Butler, whose son of the same name, promptly demolished it and rebuilt it to operate using coke. Butler expanded the firm by acquiring foundries and taking leases to work iron stone on Hunloke land with coal supplied from the same area and coked at Lings colliery. It was brought from anywhere on the first 'L' shaped wooden rails to be used anywhere above ground to a loading wharf at Ankerbold, before completing its journey by wagon to the furnace beside the stream near Belfit Hill. Coke also went from Lings colliery to Butler's foundries at Killamarsh and Stonegravels.

Not to be left out the Duke of Devonshire let a long lease to Walter Mather, who had surrendered a Hunloke lease, in order that he should rebuild the Staveley iron works. The Duke picked Mather rather than John Barnes, of Ashgate, who had a substantial mining interest at Barlow and a foundry at Stonegravels and who had wanted to expand at Staveley.

Making iron seemed like a license to print money and another opportunist was John Brocksopp of Grasshill, Grassmoor. He had inherited money from his wife, the survivor of a successful branch of the Wragg family. After over twenty years of working the Grasshill farm and mines at Hasland and Norbriggs he branched out in 1801 to build his own furnace on a small hillock at the back of Grasshill farm house. He had pioneered in this part of Derbyshire the making of coke from coal stacked in heaps but covered with the fine coke or 'breeze' made from an earlier firing. This much improved control of the ventilation to the stack and increased both the quality and quantity of coke made from Brocksopp's highly 'coyzable' coals.

The design of the furnace was like that of the furnace built by the iron master Hurt which still stands at Morley Park, Heage, alongside the Ripley bypass. The brick lined furnace was clad in stone with a tower about 35 feet high, slightly tapering, built into the side of a hill so as to provide a ramp and platform for feeding the ore and coke through a hopper top and with a run-off at the bottom into the sow and piglet moulds made of sand.

Output from Brocksopp's furnace rose steadily from 467 tons in 1801 to 914 tons in 1810. He had no foundry so his production of pig iron was sold to other foundry men like Ebenezer Smtth and John Barnes but most was sent to the cutlers of Sheffield who blended it with very high quality Swedish iron.

Sadly the honeymoon with iron making was short lived. Butler wisely decided to devote his attention to other interests after 1812, just before the post Napoleonic recession set in. Brocksopp died very suddenly in 1813 leaving only infant children and the works was mothballed and finally closed in 1830. In the same year the Griffen works of Smith was closed down though his other works, the Adelphi at Calow, struggled on for a few years. Barnes sold out and the Stonegravels foundry was closed so that Chesterfield was left without an iron industry. Robinsons acquired the Wheatbridge and Holm Brook sites of the Smiths and completely transformed them, Barnes' Stonegravels site is commemorated by the street name

'Foundry Street', Brocksopp's furnace was buried in an open cast coal mining operation and cows now graze down to the stream at Butler's Wingerworth works.

It was only the embers of an industry kept aglow at Staveley, Renishaw and later Sheepbridge, by the funding available from more profitable coal mines, that could be fanned into flames when the railways opened up new markets to once more put the district into the iron making league.

Shopping on Low Pavement

a hundred years ago

L OW PAVEMENT RUNNING ALONG THE SOUTH SIDE of Chesterfield's market square has been there, though under a number of different names, since the thirteenth century. Off it, running down to the river Hipper, that meandered then much nearer to the town, were a host of narrow burgage plots owned by the town's burgesses. On each one the owner would have built a house, endways on, and kept his cow and a few fowls on the field behind. Over the years the land was developed, first with out-houses where the owners could practise their trades, then later to house servants and other tradesmen until the whole strip, accessed through an archway, became one of the many swarming cul-de-sac yards that characterised the borough throughout the reign of Queen Victoria.

Then, as now, Low Pavement was an important shopping centre and from the 1891 population census books and the trade directories a picture can be built up of how Low Pavement looked a hundred years ago.

It started, at the Brampton end, opposite the big house occupied by the firm of solicitors, Shipton and Hallewell, with the White Horse Inn, which was to be pulled down eight years later to make way for the Lincoln, Derbyshire and East Coast Railway station. John Sydall was the landlord who had, in White Horse Yard, alongside ample stabling for his customers' horses, the yard also providing housing for thirteen families.

Towards the market the Radford and Ketton families occupied two houses between the White Horse and the Bird in Hand

public house out of whose yard the local carters Featherstone, Hage and Asman ran   regular delivery services to Walton, Ashover, Matlock, Baslow and Old Brampton.

Next door lived a very busy man, George Robinson, the vet, who cared for a vast population of horses, cows, sheep and pigs. His neighbour was Eliza Arthur but what she sold from her little shop goes unrecorded.

Dresses were made by an army of dressmakers working from their own homes but mens' suits and shirts were made up on the premises of E.D. Brown the tailor living over his shop next to Eliza's. He was glad in the freezing winters of the time to have George Firth, the plumber, as his neighbour. George would have been enjoying a boom in trade as more and more houses had water taps fitted indoors, though few houses would have had a bath plumbed in, let alone a flushed toilet.

The passageway beside the shop led down to the busy Froggart's Yard where the Blue Meeting House chapel, named after its slate roof, had stood until it was taken over as Bowker's School. Holland's lace mill, later the Alma Concert Hall and 25 houses, all to come down for the railway, also still crowded into the space.

Byron and Rangley the auctioneers and estate agents, had the next place, conveniently sited to get to the market where farmers congregated smoking and chatting waiting for the sales to start, or to get to the property sales held regularly in the Angel across the square.

Many men, and far fewer women, were smokers so Harrison the tobacconist abutting Bryon's did a brisk trade. His supplies in part would have come from Mason's tobacco factory, originally in one of the yards but later out at Spital.

The arch to the left separated the shop from the twelfth property, the prestigious Sheffield and Union Bank. This was a rather forbidding place with its mahogany sloping desks and counter resplendent with polished brass coin scales, heavy ledgers and impressive letter copying press. The grandeur concealed the rather pokey Bank Yard behind that was much smaller than the Peacock Yard next door. This took its name from the inn, which stood on a 'half-burgage' plot, (then No 68 the Pavement and now the tourist centre) where Alex Bowler was landlord.

One side of Peacock Yard close to the square was formed by J.W. Smith's corn chandler's warehouse while on the eastern side of the warehouse was the Victoria flour mill with an enormous chimney dominating the sky line. The mill yard, unlike the others, was a through lane, a bridge at the end giving pedestrian access to Boythorpe.

This was followed by Right's, the tailors, then Robinson's Yard, (each yard taking its name from the dominant occupier, and often changing names as occupiers came and went). Two grocers had the next neighbouring shops, W. Jephson to the west and R Mitchell to the east. Between them and another bank, the London and Midland, managed by John Kerns, was Eliza Revill's confectioner's.

The bank ran down the side of Prince's Yard, (named not after any royal personage, but John Prince a resident fell-monger whose festering stock must have announced its presence from afar).

Stanton and Walker, a firm of solicitors, still in practice in the town, occupied the rather charming building with its enclosed garden having as their neighbours the fourth public house the Crown and Cushion. This pub opened on to Wheldon Lane, (named after a one time occupier of the 'Peacock') which ran across the Hipper to Boythorpe.

Across the lane was the imposing surgery of J.W. Slack the dentist which abutted the premises of Ball and Friedsend the drapers renowned for their selection of lace curtains.

But by far the most outstanding building, literally and figuratively, was the Castle Inn with its pillared entry built out across the pavement to provide protection from the weather for its clients descending from their carriages. This pillared front was repeated on the central building on the north and east sides of the market square giving it an architectural balance. The inn had been built in about 1636 on the site of the house formerly occupied by Ralph Clarke the first mayor of Chesterfield. It was from here, before the railways usurped the trade, that coaches ran regularly to Birmingham.

The rest of the street was similarly pierced with entries under arches leading to many more yards, Wilcockson's, Brown's, Theatre, Ward's and others, some of which are recalled today simply by name plates. More grocers, chemists, drapers like Barker and Morley, tea blenders and cabinet makers filled the space between the Castle Inn and the Falcon. In the yards behind, Britt the iron-monger had his warehouse and Charles Haslam had a works emblazoned 'Sauce-maker to the Queen'.

The occupants have changed many times and little remains of the Low Pavement of a hundred years ago beside the well preserved facade but with a little imagination it is still possible to people the shops with aproned proprietors offering real service to their customers.

The 1938 Markham Colliery Disaster

A flashback to sixty years ago

T FIVE O'CLOCK IN THE MORNING of the tenth of May the colliers in the long row of cottages in the middle of Markham pit yard were reluctantly stirring themselves from their beds to prepare for another day shift. In the dawn light men pedalled in from Staveley and Poolsbrook and the winding engine-man got ready to wind up the night shift.

Nearly seven hundred yards underground the repair men in the Blackshale seam had finished their night's work and were starting to make their way back along the East plane tunnel to the shaft bottom. Within the next half hour almost all the men would be walking out, locking up tools, slinging water bottles over their shoulders, looking forward to a bath and getting home.

The night had been one of routine. No coal cutting machines worked on the twenty-four hour night cycle. Some roof had been ripped and new steel arches had been set. Timber had been drawn off and face conveyors had been moved over where coal had previously been loaded out. The fine coal spillage around the loading point had been cleaned up into tubs that stood with their wheels locked at the top of the incline. A whiff of firedamp from a crack in a pot-hole in the roof early in the shift had been easily dispersed by a re-alignment of a brattice cloth. Only the slow clearance of loaded tubs had raised a comment. No night shift could have been more routine and the 171 men working in the seam thought so too.

At two minutes past the half hour men nearest to the shaft,

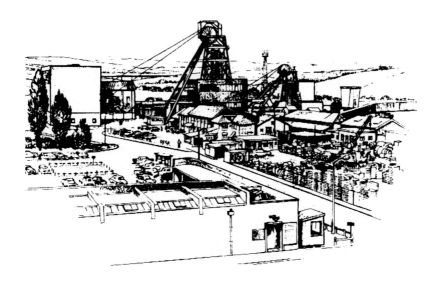

Markham Colliery

travelling down the North plane tunnel at a sharp angle from the East plane, heard a distant and ominous BUMP. In seconds it was followed by an enormous rush of air, so violent that it threw men to the ground knocking them unconscious.

In minutes the alarm was raised and word ran through the pit yard and the cottages that there had been another explosion in the Blackshale. Within 30 minutes the first rescue team was being wound into the pit and by 6.25 the Chesterfield Rescue Brigade was at the pit, followed in minutes by the Mansfield team. As the scale of the disaster was unfolded the Ilkeston Rescue Brigade was called in and rescue teams were mobilised from neighbouring collieries.

The scene that these rescuers encountered was horrendous. The violence of the explosion had buckled roof arches tearing them from their settings and hurling them into the side walls, tubs had been wrenched from the haulage cables to which they had been clipped and were piled on top of one another. Heavy air doors, intended to direct the ventilation, had been torn out and splintered so that the air flow was fatally short circuited. And strewn along the North and East planes were the lifeless bodies of the 79 men and one pony, and 40 injured men. Some had been hit by debris and caught by burns, though there had been no flame, but all had suffered or perished from carbon monoxide poisoning.

The prompt action of the rescue men in getting 40 injured men into fresh air where they received Carbogen treatment saved the lives of many who otherwise would have succumbed to the gas. Their injuries ranged from cuts and bruises to concussion and blinding headaches. But any men any distance in-bye had already died.

In the previous year there had been a firedamp explosion in the same seam and for a while tempers ran high and rumours abounded at the cause of the explosion that had cost so many men their lives.

In the ensuing long summer days a searching enquiry into the cause of the tragedy was held in the Miners' Welfare Hall, at Chesterfield, under the chairmanship of Paul Sandlands, a King's Counsel, assisted by the Chief Inspector of Mines. All those involved, the Ministry, owners, managers, officials and workmen, were represented by eminent counsel, among them Sir Stafford Cripps K.C. and Hubert Houldsworth K.C. (later to be chairman of the National Coal Board).

All readily agreed that the Staveley Coal and Iron Company, which had opened the colliery in 1882, had devoted considerable sums of money and effort into making the mine a safe place and had an efficient management team running the pit. Ventilation, particularly in the eastern part of the pit worked since 1934, had been given special attention and stone-dusting to minimise the chances of a coal dust explosion had been thorough and well above the minimum standards required by the law.

A number of theories as to the cause of the accident were advanced and carefully and fully evaluated. There was no need for a white-wash. Conditions should not have given rise to such a tragic outcome. Establishing the cause, so that action might be taken to avoid a repetition, was the essential and accepted purpose of the long enquiry.

From all the evidence presented, the Commissioner determined that this was not a fire-damp explosion but one caused by the ignition of a cloud of finely divided coal dust. The aftermath of the explosion, which consumed the available oxygen in the air, was an atmosphere of carbon monoxide in which no life could be sustained.

The location of wrecked tubs led to the conclusion that, as the men were coming out, a short train of tubs containing the fine dry sweepings from the loading point ran away down an incline and crashed from the rails piling into one another and spewing up their contents in a vapour-like curtain. This would not have been too serious had they not, as they careered down the slope, torn away an electricity supply junction box slung from the roof with such force that it broke open and tore the connecting pins apart. For some unknown reason there was a momentary electric arc in this fractured junction box which detonated the coal dust with terrifying consequences.

The enquiry recognised that coal mining was a hazardous occupation and made recommendations about the stowage of cleared up coal sweepings, the addition of more stone dust, the leaving of tubs lockered on an incline, and the making of power supply lines more secure and in consequence future practices were improved.

In Duckmanton, Poolsbrook and Staveley, where lived most of the families who had lost their men folk, life had to go on. Few homes had lost more than one member the exception being that of the Hargreaves of North Crescent, Duckmanton, where a father and two strong sons died. And although grief was shared, its shadow lay across the valley long after that cruel trick of fate some sixty years ago.

Mary Queen of Scots' arduous journeys and brief visit to Chesterfield

O N A BITTERLY ICY JANUARY DAY in 1569, under the care of her jailer, Sir Francis Knollys, Mary Queen of Scots set out with all her entourage from Bolton Castle in Wensleydale for Tutbury Castle on the Derbyshire Staffordshire border. After crossing into England as a political refugee she had been lodged at Bolton following her short stay at Carlisle Castle, but now Queen Elizabeth was concerned at the proximity of so many Scottish and Roman Catholic friends and felt security would be enhanced if Mary moved into the custody of George Talbot, 6th Earl of Shrewsbury who had so many fine midlands houses.

The 26 year old Stuart Queen was in poor health and this farcical decision taken by the Westminster conference to move her away in mid-winter from the influence of Lady Scrope, the Duke of Norfolk's sister, did nothing to improve it. Her principal companion, Lady Agnes Livingston was also unwell and really not fit to undertake so arduous a journey. But Knollys had his orders from

London and the party set off with a number of guards.

With the Queen was Lord Livingston, with his own attendants, Mary Seton, (the last of the Maries who had been the Queen's noble Scottish play-fellows) with her maid and a groom, John Beaton, the comptroller of the household (who was the grandson of a Scottish cardinal and was to die the following year, aged 32, of a dystentry at Chatsworth and be buried at Edensor), three more ladies of the bed-chamber and one Jane Kennedy a particular bed-chamber favourite of the queen. Also in the group were Willy Douglas, an usher, her secretary Gilbert Curle, her chair bearer, her cup bearer and her medical attendant. She also had the services of a master cook, a pottager, four pantry and three kitchen officials. In addition there was witty Bastion Pages, the groom of the chambers, and his wife. Other servants should have brought the number of the official complement of aides that Westminster had agreed to feed and finance up to thirty-one but in fact there were more like forty in all.

The group, like the Chaucerian pilgrims of an early age, were mounted on horses and would have hoped to cover around thirty miles a day.

The journey south, planned to take a week, was to take them through Ripon, Pontefract, Rotherham, Chesterfield, South Wingfield and on to Tutbury. At each night stage the whole company had to be found beds and be fed. And for Knollys, spared at this time the knowledge that Lady Knollys was to die in the south during the distractions of this move, there was the constant fear that an opportunity might be seized, anywhere along this isolated way across some of the most barren and god-forsaken of the English moorlands, to capture the Queen and carry her back to Scotland, or to abduct her into the arms of the Catholic Duke of Norfolk.

The bitter weather, cold and wet, took its toll. Lady Livingston soon became so ill that she could not go on and had with her servants to be left behind. The Queen also suffered and was so ill after leaving Rotherham that consideration was given to diverting to Talbot's Sheffield Castle. But this diversion could not be seriously countenanced for a messenger brought news that the castle was in too great a disarray with its hangings already transferred to Tutbury. All that could be done was to halt the cortege awhile and give the Queen some little respite to recover.

The party moved on down the River Rother valley skirting Chesterfield town and the small settlement at Brampton before coming to Walton Hall on the outskirts.

The Hall, the precursor of the building there today, which has as its core the old farm house, was a grander place built in the fourteenth century by the Foljambes around a great courtyard. This in its turn had replaced an even earlier building erected by Robert de Brito around 1160. The Foljambe mansion was impressive standing in a park of 1500 acres and a hundred years later, the Hearth Tax return shows it as having 13 fire places in use even though partially abandoned.

Though it would have been tempting to stay longer, the Queen and her retinue could only have stayed for one night pressing on the following day to Wingfield and then to Tutbury.The whole dreary journey from Bolton Castle taking just eight days.

Tutbury Castle, perhaps unbeknown to anyone at the Court in London, was in a terrible state of repair. A large part had been deserted and the occupied rooms ran with damp. Mary was appalled at the odious rooms allotted her and suffered a great deal of pain, particularly in her side after a long session of embroidering. By the end of the winter her condition worsened, her physician diagnosing a 'grief of the spleen'. Unlike Shrewsbury's intermittent fevers and pains Mary's illness was becoming chronic and remained with her to her execution at Fotheringhay.

The sixth Earl of Shrewsbury, who had taken over responsibility from Sir Francis, was not entirely without feelings and arranged after only a month for Mary to move to the more acceptable accommodation at South Wingfield Manor. This house had been partly built by Lord Cromwell and bought by the 2nd Earl of Shrewsbury in the middle of the fifteenth century. In much better repair than Tutbury it had great inner and outer courts and commodious outbuildings for servants and stables. Mary's apartments had fine views towards the Ashover valley and here she could receive visitors and write letters again to her suitor Norfolk. But even this change was insufficient to restore her health. News of the fate of some her staunchest Scottish supporters made matters worse and the young Queen's face swelled up and she would sit disconsolate and weeping.

But she was not long allowed a period for weeping. Others were plotting on her behalf. There was the reputedly treasonable correspondence with the Duke of Alva, the involvement of the Earl of Leicester and Norkolk's enemy Leonard Dacre all compounded by the Earl of Shrewsbury suffering a stroke, and his absenting himself to Buxton so that the grip on the security at Wingfield was relaxed.

News of an escape plot reached and alarmed Queen Elizabeth and once more the Scottish retinue was ordered back to the hated Tutbury where the rooms allotted Mary were even worse than at the first visit. And her conditions were further exacerbated by a reduction in her retinue and curtailment of her right to receive visitors.

Moves from Tutbury to Ashby-de-la-Zouch castle and then Coventry followed before a return to a terrible winter in Tutbury and an excruciating onset of Mary's pains.

A change of scene, with residence in yet another Shrewsbury home, was presented as a possible remedy. To this end Mary and all her entourage moved to Chatsworth in April 1570 while the castle at Tutbury was sweetened (a euphemism for the digging out of the night soil from the cess dumps that made Elizabethan houses, at times over full of guests and servants, almost uninhabitable).

This acceptable move was to the old square Chatsworth building built by Bess of Hardwick, now absorbed into the present building. Bess, herself, was to become a mother figure to the Queen the two ladies engaging in long embroidery sessions together.

But again Mary's stay was short lived and though she came back a number of times and visited Buxton to seek relief from rheumatism she never came again to Chesterfield. The stays were always short amounting to only three months out of the eleven years she was to spend as a prisoner in Sheffield Castle before her tragic last journey to the block at Fotheringhay.

The emblem of her mother, Mary of Guise, was a phoenix in flames and bore the motto 'en ma fin mon commencement'. As mamatters turned out a very suitable Stuart motto.

Skegness is So Bracing

Skegness Miners' Holiday Camp

IN 1937 THE BOLSOVER COLLIERY CO., for the first time, granted their employees a week's holiday with pay. Many of the other coal producers followed suit and the pattern of holidays taken throughout much of north Derbyshire changed for ever.

Prime mover in this change was Harry Hicken who had left school at 12 to work underground as a trammer paid ten pence a day and who had risen to be secretary of the North Derbyshire miners' trade union. His ambition was to ensure that the mine-working fraternity, men and their families, should really benefit from their new-found leisure and not just fritter it away at the street corners. His inspiration came from Billy Butlin who had just started opening his holiday camps complete with red coats, wakey wakeys and all the razzamataze of a commercial enterprise. But Harry Hicken was a strict Methodist tee-totaller who would have no truck with the evils of drink so the scheme he initiated at Skegness was a much more sober business.

The chosen site at Winthorpe Avenue had been purchased in 1925 to accommodate the first purpose built convalescent home for Derbyshire miners, replacing the rented building that had first been made available at the turn of the century by the colourful, but dubious, financier Edward Hooley who floated no fewer than 26 companies in the 1890s before going bankrupt. This land and the new wooden chalets were all paid for by funds raised by the local miners' committees with only a small grant from the Miners' Welfare Fund.

The pageant for the 1957 Ideal Holiday Girl
competition

Built close to the sea front with its great sweep of golden sand, the holiday chalets each accommodated man and wife, children sleeping in a large dormitory supervised by a nurse. Meals were served in the communal dining hall which, as the centre grew, was soon too small to seat all the 900 campers who came each week and who had to be divided into two sittings. Entertainment in the evenings and on wet afternoons was in the concert hall, professional artists often involving the amateur exhibitionists amongst the holidaying families, but Harry insisted there should be no bars on the site and the local pubs did very well out of the new establishment.

Sadly as the centre was formally opened on the 20th May 1939 by Sir Frederick Sykes the storm clouds of war were intensifying and at the end of that holiday season the whole place, including the convalescent home, was commandeered by the Army who stayed in occupation until 1946. Unfortunately they were not ideal guests and the convalescent home took some putting back into order after the War but the wooden chalets and the other core buildings were soon restored to their original purpose and once more the miners of

Derbyshire took their turn throughout the sixteen week season, each pit being given a week that rotationally changed year and year about so that each pit had a share of the best weather.

By then the mines had been nationalised and the management of the centre rested with trustees drawn from the North Derbyshire branch of the National Union of Miners and from the East Midlands Divisional Board of the National Coal Board, the chairmanship democratically changing sides each year. Their work was not onerous but they took it seriously especially when they were setting the tariffs to be charged, seeking to keep thm as low as possible.

The fees were able to be kept down because, after the War, Bert Wynn who had replaced Harry Hicken at Saltergate, persuaded the Trustees (despite objections from Harry Hicken) to seek an alcohol sales licence and soon there were some half dozen bars making substantial profits which were used as a cross subsidy.

These charges, in the early 1950s, were £5:12:6 (£5.63p.) each, for a man and wife sharing a chalet, with a charge of £1:17:6 for a baby sleeping in a cot beside them. The fees for children in the dormitory were proportionate, varying with age, from £1:17:6 to £4:12:6. To these were added the train fare, the Trustees having been able to continue the arrangements made by the private owners for special trains to run from Derbyshire to Skegness each Saturday. This whole cost of the holidays could be spread over a year, a deduction being made each week from the miners' wages.

Late in 1949, just after the end of the season, fire destroyed all the old buildings at the heart of the camp and their replacements had only just been recommissioned when in the Spring of 1953 the whole camp was put at risk by unprecedented weather. Floods inundated parts of Lincolnshire and the colossal seas broke down vital parts of the sea defences. Fortunately the warning came on Friday evening and by Saturday Herbert Dilks, the North Derbyshire N.U.M. Treasurer, had organised bus loads of miners from Markham colliery who travelled overnight to fill and build sand bag walls around the vulnerable parts of the centre. The water lapped perilously close to the top of those makeshift walls but the damage to the buildings was minimised.

The Trustees were always looking for new sources of income

and though an attempt at Christmas opening was a financial failure the centre in the winter of 1957 provided an ideal home for 400 Hungarian refugees who were being trained for work in the industry.

In its more conventional role the centre was proving even more popular than it had been before the War, but many of the mining community had experienced foreign travel during their war service and hankered after sunnier weather than even Skegness could provide. And the holiday market was just starting to expand into the Spanish resorts. To keep their clientele and meet the expectations of the mining families the Trustees realised they had to upgrade the old accommodation. So began a long capital development programme, entirely self financed, that continued over nearly three decades.

Progressively the old wooden huts were replaced with six blocks (Albert to Florence) of brick chalets, each two storeys high, with centralised showers and toilets. Then came new theatre buildings, a new dance hall, the Butterfly night club (in an under-used part of the convalescent home) and, when more land was bought from the Lincolnshire Health authority, a range of 50 self service flatlets. The crowning glory was the Drifters club opened in 1975. This building incorporated an amusement arcade, coffee bar and a mini-supermarket to supply the self service chalets and had on the first floor a sumptuous lounge bar covered from wall-to-wall with a carpet incorporating a motif of miners' lamps, helmets and picks and shovels.

The sands were always an essential ingredient of the holiday but the swimming pool and bowling green were equally popular. Many miners who had their own caravans sited near Skegness wanted to make use of these excellent facilities and it became necessary to charge an entrance fee to ration the use of the centre by such 'outsiders'. And even this arrangement brought its own difficulties, those in the second sittings for high tea complaining that all the best seats in the theatre had been taken by the outsiders before they could get in!

It was in this theatre that the camp queen competitions, sponsored by the Derbyshire Times, which presented the winner with a powder compact, were held each week. The competition was intense and not always without its moments of drama and tears. It culminated in a grand final at the end of the season when the newspaper's editor came over to Skegness to present the trophy and prize to the Ideal Holiday Girl of the year.

But as the miners' financial lot improved, the call of the Costa del Sol became greater than that of the Costa del Skegee. Pits were closing and finding ways of filling the camp, even for a shortened season, became more difficult. First the sister centre at Rhyl, which had been started soon after the War but had never been as popular as Skegness, was sold in 1978. The colliery-associated Divisions of the St John Ambulance Brigade continued to hold their week-end camps at Skegness at the start and end of the season but despite making the centre more and more available for disabled and handicapped holidaymakers, income began to fall seriously and the centre became no longer financially viable.

The final blow came in the early 1990s with the accelerated closure of the coal mines in north Derbyshire and the Trustees, very reluctantly, sold the centre to an outside commercial enterprise.

Though now the centre no longer exists , to many of the mining community the holidays at Skegee, the first and only holidays many had, remain as cherished memories: memories that may soon be lost if they are not recorded.

And much of the credit for these memories must go to Harry Hicken, who always refused to wear a tie (even when he was appointed to the N.C.B.) as a mark of his Socialism, He was not as flamboyant as Sir Billy Butlin, but his initiative in Coronation Year undoubtedly stamped the holiday patterns of a generation of the mining community of Derbyshire.

Something of an Unsung Minstrel

The story of William Newton

WILLIAM NEWTON WAS ALWAYS A MODEST, unassuming man who could not abide inhumanity. Born in December, 1750 at Cockey Farm on the wild moor between Abney and Bretton Clough he was the son of farmer George and his wife Mary.

Not wishing to follow in his father's footsteps, as he grew to manhood, he mastered the arts of carpentry helping to build local houses and repairing the fine houses in the locality. By the time he was thirty his leadership qualities had been recognised and he was employed by the Duke of Devonshire as his head carpenter at the construction of the Buxton Crescent financed by the Duke's copper mine on the Staffordshire border.

But apart from being a fine wood worker William Newton was blessed with another talent: the ability to write poetry. As he worked he turned over in his mind the lines which he would commit to paper at the end of the day. Some of his poems were published locally and while William was at Buxton they came to the attention of Anna Seward.

Anna had been born at Eyam, in the same year as William Newton, and was the daughter of the Rector of Eyam, who had transferred to be a canon of Lichfield Cathedral. She too was a writer and poet, but much more renowned, her prowess having earned her the title of 'Swan of Lichfield'. She moved in an enlightened circle enjoying the friendship of such savants as Erasmus Darwin and in later life Sir Walter Scott. Anna encouraged William to write his poetry and influenced the wider publication of his work.

Slim volumes of verse, however, never paid the rent and William and his new wife Helen were pleased to be provided with a house when he was employed to manufacture and maintain cotton-spinning machines at Arkwright's Cressbrook mill, built on the site of an old pepper-mint distillery. Fate seemed against the couple when in the winter of 1785 fire destroyed the wooden mill, festooned with cotton lint, and the adjoining houses leaving them destitute.

But Fate was not entirely evil bringing Anna Seward to the rescue. She took upon herself to persuade a number of her friends to lend money so that William could buy a third partnership share in the new mill which a man named Bossley was building on the land now leased from Richard Arkwright junior. The new mill prospered during the bonanza cotton spinning years of the 1780s so that William Newton was able to repay in full his debts to Anna Seward.

For some unknown reason William gave up his partnership and was quickly plunged into bankruptcy. For a short time he maintained his family by working in Cheshire and was delighted to be recalled to Cressbrook to manage the mill.

Unlike the mills of Arkright at Crompton, Jedediah Strutt at Belper and Evans at Darley Abbey which could draw on local child and female labour, the mills in the remoter areas around Litton and Cressbrook relied on pauper apprentices drawn from the poor law orphanages of London. At some of the mills these poor children, some as young as seven or eight, were cruelly treated, ill fed and were worked for inhumanely long hours. But Newton's approach was outstandingly different. He provided good housing, wholesome food and ensured the children had eight hours sleep. This humanity was carried on by his descendants who are still remembered in Tideswell with affection. It is fortunate that a drawing of him done by Francis Chantrey, who was invited into the Newton house while walking in Monsal Dale, still survives.

William Newton rode out the bad cotton years at the end of the French wars and prospered. In his seventies he built a new mill, the glorious Georgian building which still stands at the end of Monsal Dale.

Although William Newton is remembered as a cotton king he can also claim to have made his mark in history by eliminating a barbaric practice. He had been named 'Minstrel of the Peak' when Anna Seward was promoting his poetic works and as such had a reasonably wide audience. Most of his poetry, which is in a somewhat affected, classical style, was not in any way controversial except for one poem, perhaps the best known, in which he rails against the practise of gibbeting felons hanged for murder.

The poem was inspired by the gibbeting of Anthony Lingard hanged for the murder of the toll keeper, Hannah Litton. His body was hung in chains at the toll House Wardlow Mires in March 1815. Incredibly large crowds came to see the rotting body and the site became like a fair ground with refreshment stalls and fortune tellers. Newton was appalled at the spectacle and the verse he wrote was instrumental in rousing a public outcry so voluble that it made this the last gibbeting of a felon in England; though the reputed cost of £100 may have weighed more heavily with the enforcers of the law.

William retired to Tideswell where he wrote some tranquil sonnets before his death, aged eighty, and was buried on the north side of Tideswell Church, the 'Cathedral of the Peak'.

The wish of the last lines of one of his last sonnets was surely achieved by a man, who, through all life's vicissitudes, retained his commitment to humanity:

'So let me, in life's tranquil evening, find
Calm, soft, unruffled joys, and sunshine of the mind.'

The Potteries of Brampton Moor

THE OLD MAN SPAT ON HIS HANDS and shovelled the last of the heavy grey clay from the weathered heap into the cart. It was the last load of the day and he was turning over in his mind the news he'd heard on his last delivery to Briddons earlier in the day. The River Alma had been crossed and our boys had won a battle. He'd no idea where the Crimea was but he was glad we'd won.

They set off from East Moor, the horse straining up the short rise, then holding back the load the whole way down the hill before the pull across Brampton Moor. The township was almost completely hidden in the haze of smoke from the dozen or so pot kilns, but its presence was felt in the increasingly acrid taste of sulphur and chlorine.

Kilns had been part of the Brampton scene for over a hundred years and the village had a reputation for turning out coarse stone earthenware made from the local potters' clay taken from the moor which even went back to the fifteenth century. As the local clay was partially worked out later in the nineteenth century it was supplemented with clay brought down by carters from East Moor and Stonedge. Fuel for the kilns came from coal and coke made at Boythorpe and Brampton and some brought over from Grassmoor and Hasland.

The products were fairly utilitarian and though no Wedgewood inspired the making of artistically satisfying pieces the output matched the market demand and the potters flourished. The wide range of cooking and dairy pots and dishes, in plain pale brown, had given way in part to the manufacture of salt-glazed coffee and teapots, tastefully decorated with sprigs depicting pastoral and patriotic scenes. These sprigs were cast in plaster of

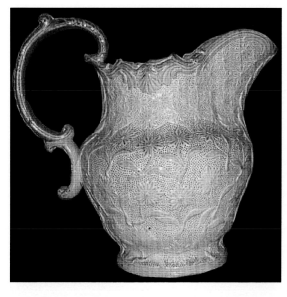

Paris moulds that dried out the slip and made it possible to attach the decoration and fire it onto the pot. With the extension of the water supply in Chesterfield and towns throughout England the demand for water filters grew and were added to the range of bakers' or loaf pots. Decoration was enhanced by dipping the green pots in a ferruginous slip to give a shoulder deep dark brown glaze which made them prized by users in Paris and Hamburg. The salt glazing made the pot impervious to moisture and was achieved by throwing common salt into the hot kiln, a hazardous and unpleasant process which led to some pots being more proofed than others and the environment being more than a little polluted.

Markets came and went but just as demand for some products was flagging a new demand arose for stoneware preserve jars when the jam trade was stimulated by a Continental subsidy on sugar that brought cheap sugar flooding into Britain. In close pursuit came the demand for stoneware ginger beers bottles and wine jars covered in woven willow strips. And fairly constantly there was a demand for puzzle jugs. These were jars, intended for liquors of any proof, that had a number of short spouts scattered about them. Liquid would run from many spouts, drenching the drinker, or from none at all, frustrating the drinker, unless the appropriate spouts were blocked off with the drinker's fingers.

These booming markets, principally supplied only wholesale, kept the pug mills and throwing wheels, the drying sheds, heated by smoky stoves, and the seven kilns, (two round and five long burning kilns), at Barkers', busy from morning to dusk, while the kilns went on giving a faint glow to the night sky.

Barkers' was a relatively new comer. Much older were the potteries of the Briddon family, Samuel, Henry and William, started in the 1830s, and those of Luke and Matthew Knowles all of whom had also at some stage

made bricks and tiles. The Robinsons operated a pottery at Wheatbridge for a short period in the 1750s before leasing it to Edward Wright & Co. and Pearsons had kilns on what is now the site of Safeways. The London Pottery built by Lipscombe went into production in the mid 1860s being taken over by James Pearson who also acquired Oldfield's Pottery before selling it to J.J. Blow. As the generations moved on potteries came and went: The Walton Pottery, The Welshpool Pottery, Lowe's Alma and Brunswick Pottery and Payne's.

Although the Barker Lane potteries of the Briddons and the Beehive Pottery in the yard behind lasted for over a hundred years, the Barker Lane works only closing in 1957, their demise became inevitable with the increasing use of glass for bottling and a demand for more delicate ware for use from oven to table.

Now there are no more than the scars of the clay holes on East Moor and the long ramshackle drying sheds and packing warehouses have gone but the surviving pieces of the potters' art are much sort after by collectors attracted by some of the delicate sprig work on what was intended to be just work-a-day brown Bristol ware. Even the old carter's plain brown beer jar would have its place in an antiques fair.

Chesterfield Royal Hospital

In the footsteps of Florence Nightingale

THE 28TH OF SEPTEMBER 1859 was a crisp autumn day and an air of expected carnival permeated the town. The Mayor of Chesterfield was at the market hall early to welcome his important guests, including the Duke of Devonshire and his eldest son and many other dignitaries to a lavish breakfast served in the Assembly Room.

At his behest all the shops in the town had been closed from an hour before noon to three o'clock so that the trades people of the town could witness the procession and formal laying of the foundation stone for the new hospital by the Marquis of Hartington.

The hospital, to be erected in front of the school board school in Durrant Road faced Holywell Cross on what had been part of the Durrant estate. The design, to match utility with architectural elegance, taxed the trustees who laboured long and hard over whether they could afford to dress the corner of the building with stone quoins at an extra cost of £50. Fortunately elegance won.

The new building replaced dispensary and hospital, close to the parish church in St. Mary's Gate that had served the poor of the town for the previous six years. There some thirteen in-patients (ten of whom recovered) were treated in its first year of operation while nearly twenty times as many were dispensed drugs as out patients, The Dispenser had a paid appointment but there were no paid surgeons, the medical services being provided free by local general practitioners, for the approach to medical services was very different in the mid-Victorian period.

Middle-class patients would engage a live-in nurse and be treated at home and only the poor, requiring surgery, would use the dispensary's services. To do so they had to get nomination from a 'responsible person' and pay two shillings (10p) a week (as a contribution to the cost of their board) before going into hospital. Failure to pay led to immediate discharge. These admission rules applied in the new hospital which was managed by a full time Matron handsomely paid £25 a year with all her keep found, provision being made for her accommodation , storage and a small operating theatre on the first floor.

The hospital had been designed in the best Nightingale manner to provide as much light and ventilation as possible- the wards being long rooms heated by open coal fires. Privacy was an invention of the middle class that was hardly shared by the patients in the 20 bedded wards where the sexes were sternly separated, At the outset the poor, perhaps not surprisingly, hated the prospect of going into hospital to face treatment with the knife and some twenty years were to pass before the new working class more readily accepted the services offered and became very important financial contributors to its success.

During the whole of this early period no medical cases were admitted because there was a real concern that the beds would soon be taken up by long-stay cases of tuberculosis and other chronic diseases.

But as the population grew new accommodation was essential and it came from the endowments of benefactors whose benevolence was enshrined in the ward names: Devonshire, Portland, Manvers and Pearson (which took over the old board school). At the same time specialist departments were developed: radiography, ophthalmology and ear, nose and throat . The domestic services, previously in the basement, were re-housed with a new laundry built on more Durrant land behind Holywell House after the old deserted chapel on Durrant Road had been pressed into service.

By 1908 funds were available to build a nurses' home that served the hospital for seventy years. Finding such funds to keep the hospital running and provide better facilities was a constant problem. It was partially solved in the early part of the century by introducing a system of workmen's weekly subscriptions which divided the clientele into contributors and non-contributors, the former having a right of access but the latter still needing the recommendation of a 'responsible person' before receiving treatment, other than in a dire emergency.

But members of the community were always generous. The coal owners and ironmasters recognised the contribution made by the hospital to the welfare of their workforces, with Barnes, of the Grassmoor Colliery Company , organising the financing of a ward as did Charles Markham of the Staveley Coal and Iron Company. By the First World War the hospital was capable of giving a good medical service to the town but the war brought serious problems. The three shillings a day paid by the War Office for each casualty treated was a welcome financial help but it did not compensate for the loss of subscriptions as men were called up and family incomes fell dramatically. At the same time labour became difficult to find just as pressure to treat casualties from the Front filled the wards and corridors to over-flowing . It was in recognition of the stalwart way in which the hospital functioned in this critical period that earned the title of Royal, bestowed by King George V in 1919.

After the war there was a further expansion that congested the site. The borough was responsible for the provision of maternity services and to provide them it built a considerable new block, emblazoned with the borough crest, and opened in the early nineteen twenties.

By 1924 the new Staveley ward was fitted with central heating from water pipes, though the rest of the wards still used open fires and the generosity of Mr. Murphy saw the opening of another ward.   As the Second World War approached the creaking bureaucratic government structure was more and more found to be wanting. Even the most routine decisions were taken by endless committees, and then ratified by many more. And there was still the stigma of the 'necessitous poor'- the non-contributors. But the proposals made by the Beveridge Report to nationalise the service were not initially welcomed with any enthusiasm. There was opposition that local management, who knew local needs, would be swept away and the sense of responsibility of the people of the town for their own 'voluntary hospital' would be lost.

Beveridge won and in due course the new Royal Hospital at Calow, this time opened by by Queen Elizabeth, replaced the worn-out site at Holywell Cross. Fortunately for the town, the core building for which the Marquis of Hartington laid the foundation stone on that crisp Autumn day has not been lost, but has been reopened as a handsome new office block with a new lease of life.

The Birth of the Borough

THE COURSE OF HISTORY for the burgesses of Chesterfield wishing to be responsible for their own local government was not simple right from the granting of the Charter by King John to William Brewer. Unlike the Charters granted direct to the burgesses of Derby and Nottingham, that of Chesterfield was granted to an individual land not to the corporation and despite several 'confirmations' the matter was not clearly resolved. To add to the problems the lords of the manor were often powerful persons, and wealthy landlords exercised their sway and cramped the style of the ambitious tradesmen.

But the impact which the likes of the Foljambes and Heathcotes had on the development of the town of Chesterfield into a corporate borough paled into insignificance compared with that of the Talbots Earls of Shrewsbury.

The Talbots (who had considerable estates in Stafford) had steadily increased their wealth and by the start of the 16th century had acquired large estates close to Sheffield, where they wished to establish their main seat. Included was the manor of Chesterfield, acquired in 1518, and a number of town properties.

During the 15th century the burgesses of Chesterfield, largely through default of the lord, had accessed the income arising from many aspects of manorial activity. During the lordship of Francis, the fifth Earl, this state of affairs went unchallenged. His son George, who succeeded in 1560, and was soon to be burdened with the costs of confining Mary Queen of Scots, was far more money conscious. He at once put in hand a detailed survey of all his land holdings which revealed that the burgesses of Chesterfield, despite their voluble objections, had no legal claim to the gild incomes they had appropriated. The upshot was that the lease for the properties was taken over by the sixth Earl who denied the burgesses any rights to self government.

For a while the burgesses, smarting from being called 'arrant knaves' by Shrewsbury, lay low being well aware of the Earl's propensity to use strong arm tactics when rebuffed. They re-opened their claim with caution. An extraordinarily bitter encounter ensued in January 1567 when the Earl summoned their representatives to a meeting at his castle in Sheffield. The burgesses' supplications were angrily received, they were trounced and sent away with a flea in their ears. To make matters even more painfully plain, a year later the Earl, now living apart from his wife Bess of Hardwick, confirmed that they had no rights to self government.

The abject position of the burgesses, so much at odds with their expectations from earlier charters, which had ostensibly granted them 'free rights', stemmed from the failure to obtain a royal charter of incorporation direct from the Crown.

The prospect looked bleak until Nicholas Clarke, in 1584, offered to take up their cause. He promised to obtain a better deal and greater freedoms than had originally been enjoyed but they had agreed not to press him on how he was going to perform this miracle.

Clarke was of a local family who had made his money as an attorney at Clement's Inn. He had bought an estate at Somersall where he had built a sizeable mansion. Although the burgesses knew that Clarke had previously been an officer of the Talbots when the burgesses lost their lease, they agreed to his plan, Clarke arguing that the Earl was getting old and was out of favour at Court.

Clarke presented his case at the Court of Augmentations and by dubious pleading succeeded in getting the gild lands' lease assigned to his three sons agreeing to pay the burgesses four times the amount paid annually by the Shrewsburys, but still much less than the £40 a year they had enjoyed before 1560. This chicanery did not go down well with the Chesterfield burgesses and, worse still, it infuriated the Earl who sent in his heavy gang to harass his Chesterfield tenants, some of whom were evicted and violently abused - so violently that their lives was feared for and prayers were said for their survival at the parish church.

The Earl's cattle in great numbers were driven into the gild fields to devour the grass and deny it to other graziers. Horses were driven out of the gild field and injured and dogs were set to chase the townsfolks' sheep. There was no doubt about the Earl's venom.

The conflict rumbled on, George Talbot bringing a court action against Clarke. Clarke was put in the Marshalsea Gaol and was released only when it was decided there was no case to answer. Only the death of Clarke, followed soon after by the demise of the Earl in 1590, brought this soap opera saga to a close.

The final analysis showed Clarke had in no way improved the rights of the burgesses, but his sons had gained a sizeable property portfolio, and the Earl was left in a richer and stronger position than in 1560.

The burgesses now turned to moré direct action to obtain a royal charter. How it was engineered is uncertain. The only records leading up to the grant by Queen Elizabeth in 1598 notes that it cost eight score pounds 'beside heavy travail' and that the Earl's steward disapproved of the townsfolks' scheming to overthrow his master's right to the town he had enjoyed from 'time out of mind'.

The new charter established the office of Mayor, the first occupant by perversity, another Clarke , Ralph, who with his alderman formalised a system of local government where the ruling clique became virtually self perpetuating. It was drawn from the wealthier and influential lead merchants, mercers, tanners, butcher-graziers and braziers: the Clarkes, Heathcotes, Websters, Bretlands and Wheldons, while the Lord of the Manor, Talbot, took no more than a paternalistic role

The burgesses had won their struggle but it would be another two and a half centuries before anything like democratic local government came into the hands of Chesterfield's townspeople.

Mortar, Mortar everywhere

Brickmaking

ALMOST ALL THE HOUSES IN CHESTERFIELD are constructed of brick, the majority having been built in the Victorian or Edwardian period. But the use of bricks for building was not the norm for this part of the county until after the canals and railways made for cheap transport. Stone was the architects' natural choice for buildings north of a line running roughly across the county from Ashbourne to Long Eaton, while brick building was confined to south of that line. Indeed today it is almost impossible to find a grand house built in the north of the county other than in stone. Only the elegant three bayed Longstone Hall at Great Longstone, built by Thomas Wright in 1747, and Castle Hill House at Bakewell built in 1785, stand out as unusual Peakland phenomena although Barlborough Hall was built in stuccoed brick in 1584.

Good building stone and timber were readily available in the Peak and were the natural choice for builders. They erected the common stock with timber frames and wattle-filled panels (as can still be seen upstairs in the Peacock tourist centre in Chesterfield) and they sculpted the grand houses from the useful variety of building stone. But by the early part of the eighteenth century brick was starting to become fashionable and houses were being erected with stone at the rear and sides but with a front elevation of brick, possibly with quoins and window dressing in ashlar stone. So desirable was brick that that it attracted an excise duty from the 1740s to 1851.

Stylish brick built houses such as Bladon Castle, Sudbury Hall. Repton Grange and Bentley Hall certainly abounded in the south of Derbyshire. At these, the bricks were most probably made on site from local clays or marls that were highly suitable for brick making. The process was long and tedious. First the clay was dug and carted in autumn to be stacked in low heaps on open ground. During the winter, if it was cold enough, frost would break it up into a crumbly mass that could be moved in late spring into a shallow basin dug out of the ground. Here a measured quantity of water would be added as the clay was trodden by men, women and children into a stiff plastic mass. This heavy product was next carted to the brickmakers, who moulded the green bricks in wooden forms, from where they were barrowed to be laid out in rows in the drying area. By the late summer when they were free of most inherent moisture they had to be stacked ready for baking. This firing process was a bit like that adopted for charcoal making. A layer of of old bricks about nine inches thick would be spread on the floor as a bed to stop damp rising, the channels, flues, of small coal would be laid along this base. The dried green bricks were then stacked around the fuel, more flues being left for air to circulate. The whole stack was finally covered with more old bricks and soil to keep the heat in. Once the fuel was fired the air flow was controlled to give a low temperature at first to drive off the remaining moisture and then a much higher temperature to bake the bricks, the cooking period being about three weeks. The product would vary considerably in quality. The best bricks would have been correctly burnt and even in colour but others would be distorted, over- or under-burnt. But all would find a use as path material or at worse as rubble in-fill.

This cumbersome process served well enough when building great houses, each year generating enough bricks for the ensuing season's building programme, but by the mid-1700s the demand for bricks was growing rapidly at a time when civil engineering works were proliferating even more rapidly, over three million bricks, for example, being needed to line the Chesterfield canal tunnel at Norwood.

The process, up to baking, was as old as that practised by the Sumarians (who made sun dried bricks) and the Egyptians (who blended them with straw) and remained virtually unchanged until the system started to be mechanised in the 1750s. Horse-power was applied to mortar machines which allowed the clay to be pulverised whatever the weather and, a century later, steam power replaced horse power while the newly designed pug mill puddle, the old upright stack, was replaced by the clay ready for the brickmaker and took out the drudgery of trampling. The old updraught stack was replaced by a brick built kiln which had the fuel burning beneath an oven so that the fuel and bricks were kept apart and a better make of bricks resulted.

It was this type of steam-powered brickworks that was opened in the 1830s by Richard Elliott at Brampton Moor, James Gratton at Stonegravels and Rawlinson and Elliott in the heart of Chesterfield town at Church Lane, successors to the long-forgotten; brickmakers now only remembered in the alley named Brick Lane, which joins Marsden and Spencer streets.

These works met the town's needs but its growth, following the opening of the railways and the collieries, attracted Henry Priestley, a master brickmaker from Barnsley who saw the opportunity in this market and opened a brickworks at the Brushes, which worked profitably from 1872 until it closed in the early part of the First World War. It was more mechanised and, with the aid of its moulding machine, a brickmaker aided by a boy, could turn out over ten thousand green bricks a week. These would be laid out to dry for just three weeks before being fired in one of the three kilns to make facing or over- or under-burnt common bricks, many in a variety of shapes ranging from the standard oblong to bullnosed or egg-ended. But the Priestleys prided themselves that they never made down-market wire-cut bricks.

Even with five other works at Sheepbridge, Unstone and Whittington and the Byron works at Bolsover, the demand for bricks could not be met. Collieries like Bolsover and Grassmoor (making 14,000 bricks a day) which had initially built brickworks, using the highly suitable clays found below the coal seams and the almost limitless supply of small coal to make bricks for their underground needs, were able to divert bricks into the property market. The output being classically used to build the model villages at Bolsover and Creswell.

During the 1920s the house building market stagnated and although some colliery brickworks continued to work, most local works closed with the movement to large centralised companies as motor transport made bricks mass-produced, in continuously operating kilns, much cheaper. The local works progressively disappeared and all that now recalls them is the name of the maker embossed in the frog (the indentation in the top of the brick) occasionally seen when an old wall is pulled down.

Drunk for a Penny

Dead drunk for tuppence, Clean straw for nothing

WHILST RELIGION MAY, in Karl Marx's view, have been the opium of the people in the industrial age, gin had played this role half a century earlier as the sign over the shops proclaimed. But the good burgesses of Chesterfield had no reason to turn to spirits when the ale they brewed was of so renowned a quality.

The ale wives of the town had brewed beer for family consumption and sale for longer than anyone cared to remember and the quality of their brew was sampled and checked regularly by an official ale taster. It was evidently up to scratch when that indomitable traveller, Celia Fiennes, visited the town at the end of the eighteenth century and commented not only on the cheapness of pullets bought in the market but recorded that 'in this town is the best ale in the Kingdom, generally esteemed'.

Licensing of alehouses goes back to 1495, though most licences were issued under an Act passed fifty-seven years later. Application for a license to sell ale was made by the inn keepers, then delightfully known as 'the tipplers', to a special 'brewster session' of the magistrates when the constable presented a list for approval.

Strictly, ale houses were places where beer was drunk on the premises, their openness proclaimed by the door jambs being painted blue or blue stoops being placed outside. Inns, on the other hand, also provided accommodation for travellers. While inns were found in towns and along travelling routes, ale houses tended to cluster in towns to a density in Chesterfield of one ale house for every five or six private households. The inns also provided rooms for public meetings: the regular meetings in 1776 of the committee appointed to manage the affairs of the company of proprietors of the Canal Navigation from Chesterfield to the River Trent being held in the house of Mr Cowley, the Angel Inn, or the house of Mr John Saxton, the Castle Inn, Chesterfield.

Hogarth's 'Rake's Progress' illustrates how excessive drinking became a national problem and with increasing industrialisation the Government felt it had to act to curb the wantonness of the poor by encouraging a return to beer rather than spirit drinking. It was with this intent that the Beerhouse Act of 1830 became law.

The Act made it legal for any householder to apply for an excise license which would allow them to brew and retail beer from their premises. These two guinea licenses did not turn out well for the newly named beerhouses, for, unlike the full license premises, they were not under the control of the magistrates and the multitude of outlets became very rowdy places. Full licences covered the retail sale of beer, cider, spirits, wines and sweets, the latter being any liquor made from fermented fruit and sugar, and were only granted to reasonably conducted premises. The oval plaque of 1791 on the re-built Square and Compass in West Bars recalls that the licensee was authorised to deal in foreign spirits and liquors. Such conditions prevailed until another Act in 1869 brought the beerhouses under control of the magistrates and new licences became increasingly difficult to obtain.

Despite these measures drunkenness continued to be a problem although many non-conformist groups and the Rechabites did their best to get signatories to the pledges of abstention. The beginning of the present century saw more moves to curtail the number of licences and the payment of compensation, financed by a levy on the licensed victuallers, when licences were not renewed.

Retaining a license could be a tricky business, for the 1869 Act required a beerhouse to remain open, without exception, for every session. Rebuilding or extending a public house thus became a logistical nightmare. To get round the problem, the Blue Bell on Holywell Cross was rebuilt behind the old pub and the Turf Tavern was replaced by the Punch Bowl built behind it. And when the new railway warranted the construction of the Portland Hotel this had to be phased in two stages, one taking up the site of the Bird in Hand

and the other the neighbouring White Horse whose licence was first transferred to the new hotel next door.

Many of these inns were used by the nascent trade union movement for their meetings, the Three Tuns being used for the 1861 meeting which brought the South Yorkshire Miners' Association into Derbyshire, and the Freemason's Arms, on Newbold Road, being home to the first delegate meeting of colliery lodges in 1876 to form the North Derbyshire Miners' Association. And again in 1893 the Queen's Head was the venue chosen for the formation of a Trades Council in 1893 which brought a number of unions into one confederacy.

The location of Chesterfield's public houses frequently changed, some retaining an old name while others took new names. And some simply disappeared from the scene. Thus the Angel, which had stabling for 40 horses and a yard stretching from the market square to Saltergate, was destroyed by fire in 1917 and re-appeared as a new house on Derby Road a few years later. In contrast there was no phoenix-like resurrection for the Bricklayers Arms that stood on South Street (and gave way to a grocery store) nor the Exchange Inn which was cleared away as part of the car park on Holywell Street.

Well over a hundred public houses have been identified in the centre of Chesterfield in the previous century, of which about a third were simple beerhouses and two thirds fully licensed premises. Not all existed at the same time but they certainly provided enough drinking time to give Chesterfield the reputation of being one of the rowdiest towns in Britain.

Today drinking and driving laws have curtailed the number of public houses in the centre of Chesterfield to around thirty, all fully licensed, the old beerhouses having completely disappeared.

The imbibing of a beverage, made by fermenting honeycomb and water and called by the Romans cerevisia, has come a long way but the refreshing draught of Midlands beer is just as pleasurable albeit not so cheap as 'drunk for a penny, dead drunk and straw tuppence'.

Pennies from Heaven

Samuel Fox

ON A WARM SUMMER'S EVENING the bells of St Barnabas church, Bradwell, rang out over the hills of north Derbyshire. But the sound that drifted towards Whin Hill was not entirely melodious, for the tenor bell was worn and slightly flat.

Across the road from the church a lad stood at the open door of his father's workshop behind their ivy clad cottage. He was Samuel Fox. His father was turning spindles which he sold to the bump-mill in the neighbouring village of Edentree. Samuel wondered if his destiny also lay in sleepy Bradwell, the home of lead miners, cotton and silk spinners and weavers. Bump, coarse cotton, came in from Liverpool and silk was brought from as far away as Southampton....places as remote as the man-in-the-moon. If only he could get away?

Samuel had been born in the month of the battle of Waterloo, and he thought his chance to see the world had come when still only a boy he was apprenticed to the wire finishing trade at Hathersage.

The wire came from Sheffield and Barnsley and was made in a multitude of small workshops, sometimes using water power to turn a wheel, but more often manually by cranking a handle that pulled red-hot iron or steel through a hole, cleverly tapered in an iron plate called a wortle. By this method iron could be reduced to a fine filament.

At Hathersage the wire might be further drawn and then be cut and ground to make needles, fish hooks, awl blades, and the porcupine-like spikes used to make tools to card cotton or raise the nap on fine wool.

The grinding was carried out in long stone-built sheds, the rows of grinding wheels driven by water power. The wages the grinders earned, bent all day over their racing stones, were good but their expectations of life were short. From time to time the gyrating wheels burst without any warning causing terrible mutilation, if not de-capitation, of the grinder. And as if this was not hazard enough the fine dust from the gritstone grinding wheels inhaled all day turned the workers' lungs to stone.

It was in such a shed that Samuel Fox spent the first half of his apprenticeship before transferring to complete it in Sheffield, learning the art of wire drawing.

He learnt the craft well, and though the early 1830s were a period of industrial and agricultural depression, with farmers unable to pay their rents, the young Samuel was soon in partnership competing in the wire trade.

At twenty-seven he was ready to take off on his own account. He was married and his wife was a source of great support for him, competent at keeping the books of account and dealing with the banks. They made their first business move by buying the site and buildings of the old grinding mill joiners' shop and cotton mill at Stocksbridge, converting them into a new wire drawing works. He already had established markets but now started to experiment in the methods of drawing hollow steel wire and perfecting a way of making it flexible.   The outcome of his experiments was the ability to manufacture fine strong steel wire that he patented turning one of its uses to the making of umbrella ribs. Such was the birth of Fox's Patent Paragon umbrella.

Umbrellas had been around from the earliest days of Chinese history and had long been the mark of royalty in the Siamese peninsular, but most such silk umbrellas, coloured according to rank, were fixed, not collapsible on their poles .Folding umbrellas were used in late Elizabethan times, but became popular, more against the rain than to provide shade in the late eighteenth century. Only though they were technically   'folding' they were extremely cumbersome, with ribs made of wood or cane, or even whale-bone. Their bulk was perhaps epitomised by Fred Barnard's illustrations of the brolly of the loquacious nurse, Sairey Gamp, in Dickens' Martin Chuzzelwit, her name moving into the language just as Samuel Fox was altering the concept.

His patent Paragon frame was soon selling all over the world and for a short while the hollow wire also found a market providing hoops for ladies' crinolines, though with the change in fashion this latter use was short lived.

The factory in Stocksbridge grew in size and Fox built his own private Stocksbridge railway, over a mile in length, to link it to the main line and save him the burden of transporting raw materials in and his finished products out. The mainstay of the business had been the steel ribbed frame, but his ingenuity soon took him into the manufacture of of winding ropes for the burgeoning deep-mined coal industry and wires for the new telegraph service.

By his death early in 1852 he had established a business employing over 2,000 people and so well-founded was it that by the end of the Second World War it was employing three times that number.

All through his life he had remembered his own humble beginnings and was generous in making anonymous gifts to the poor and giving the sons of Bradwell apprenticeships to aid them strike out on their own. His thousand pounds bequest set up a charity that still continues to provide help for the needy in his old village.

It was fitting that just before the War his niece, Fanny Jeffrey, should have funded a new peal of bells at St. Barnabas, so that now in June, when the shade of a parasol is welcome, the clamour of distant bells heard towards Whin Hill is once more in tune.

Graven Images

The Monumental Brasses of Derbyshire

I T IS FORTUNATE that the parish church of Chesterfield famous for its crooked spire contains a fine example of a monumental brass, dating from 1529, depicting the knightly Sir Godfrey Foljambe and his wife Katherine, for Derbyshire, as a whole, is not notably well endowed having only about 25 such brasses.

The practice of fastening engraved memorial plates to the church floor or over the tombs of the departed, which was very much a continental custom, grew out of the use of altar-tombs. These in the early twelfth century had been replaced by bas-relief effigies on the lids of coffins and then by incised stone slabs. The materials used to make the heavy plates, copper and zinc, made them expensive status symbols of the rich. The more so since their manufacture was a monopoly of Germany and the Low Countries so that all of them had to be imported.

It was this Low Countries source of supply that accounts for by far the largest number of surviving memorial brasses being in churches in the counties of East Anglia and Kent, easily accessible by sea. Varying but smaller numbers are found as one goes west and north from the eastern seaboard until, in Wales and Scotland, there are virtually none. There would, in all probability, be many more had not the intrinsic value of the metal encouraged many of the puritanical rebels during Cromwell's Civil War and Commonwealth not only to desecrate but also remove many wholesale, in much the same way as they were later to be vandalised in France during the Reign of Terror.

The earliest of these cullen or latten plates, as they were known, were beautifully engraved, some by continental craftsmen. They were coloured with enamel like materials which over the years have been worn away by the passage of many feet. But some used real enamel and this remains as pristine as ever giving a rare insight into how decorative the originals must have been. Over the years the plain plates were imported and worked by local craftsmen whose skill was not always so well developed as that of the early engravers. Indeed as the years progressed the quality of workmanship steadily declined. The cullen sheets were much thinner and many sheets were 'salvaged' or were partially worked 'seconds' which were either cut up or simply turned over to be reused as palimpsests. By the middle of the Tudor period the status value was on the decline and relatively few brasses date from the seventeenth century.

But it was this status quality that accounts for the earliest examples being of wealthy ecclesiastics in their ceremonial vestments, or knights depicted in full armour, lying with an armorial animal at their feet or standing with their long swords hanging diagonally from their belts. Often they are flanked by their wife, or wives, and sometimes they are accompanied by miniature cut-outs of their children and an amorial hatchment. From their knightly attire it is possible to glean much about changes that occurred in the design of armour starting in England with the earliest of such brasses, dating from 1277. This commemorates Sir John D'Aubernoun, life sized, with his enamelled armorial hatchment still brightly coloured. His armour is markedly differently from that of John Stathum buried nearly two hundred years later and appearing on the oldest Derbyshire plate at Morley. He lies close to his kinsman, and is shown together with his three wives. Different again are the four members of the Eyre family lying in Hathersage church with memorials covering a hundred years from 1463, or that of Sir Henry Sacheverell in full Elizabethan armour at Morley. And it is not only the men that are of interest, the wife of Nicholas Kniveton, engraved on a brass at Muggington, dating from the end of the fifteenth century, is of particular interest since she is shown with long flowing hair, a style normally reserved only for unmarried women. Fortunately, in Derbyshire, we are spared the imagery of mortality, the skeleton or shrouded remains that became the hall mark of the late Elizabethan period memorial.

But, as the practice of adopting sepulchral monuments became more popular, it was not only knights, bishops and monks that were depicted. By the fifteenth century many successful professionals, lawyers, administrators and even tradesmen, vintners, mercers and haberdashers and humble widows were being remembered. Frequently their engraved effigies were coupled with emblems representing their trade guilds incorporated with an inscription around the border of the plate. Among such is the plate of Elizabeth Porte, the only widow to be commemorated in Derbyshire, on a memorial at Etwell. Widowhood was distinguished by showing the lady dressed in a kirtle, stylised for many centuries and accompanied by a gorget of finely pleated cloth drawn closely to the chin or by including a long veil.

The male civilian, Latham Woodroofe, appears on a brass at Bakewell and, dating from around 1500, Robert Lytton, dressed in a long gown, with his demure wife Isabel beside him is depicted on a small brass at Tideswell. And whilst elsewhere, in other parts of the country, a number of academics, lawyers, abbots, monks, and nuns are commemorated, there are none in Derbyshire. Only three priests, dressed in chasubles, are recorded at Dronfield, Walton-on-Trent and Ashover. And fortunately there is one fine example of a bishop in ceremonial vestments (which remained virtually unchanged over four centuries) the last of the pre-reformation bishop's memorial brasses surviving in Britain, which is to be found at Tideswell. It commemorates Robert Pursglove, Suffragan Bishop of Hull and is dated 1579. He is of particular interest because he is depicted wearing the low mitre which was worn by bishops for over two hundred and fifty years before the reign of Charles I when mitres started to be much taller.

And though there is only one ancient brass in the county commemorating a bishop Chesterfield parish church has a very fine example of a modern memorial brass commemorating an archbishop. This is to Geoffrey Clayton who was vicar of Chesterfield in the ten years from 1924 and archbishop of Cape Town from 1948 to 1957.

The Crystal Palace and Great Exposition of 1851

IN 1849 A COMMITTEE was appointed to oversee the staging of the world's grandest exhibition. Its first task, which was to agree the design of a building of gigantic proportions that would house all the promised exhibits, was nearly its undoing. Local residents objected strongly to the erection of any building in Hyde Park and were only pacified by assurances that the structure would be temporary and would be removed to another site as soon as the exhibition was over. The international invitation for designs resulted in all 245 proposals being rejected by the committee which then decided to do the design work itself. The result was the inevitable monstrous camel with a central unedifying dome the sad design of no less an engineer than Brunel, so that the future of the Great Exhibition hung in the balance.

Salvation came in the person of Sir Joseph Paxton, a self-made man, who had been encouraged by the Duke of Devonshire while he was the head gardener to design and build a magnificent conservatory at Chatsworth. It was this elegant and ingenious design using cast iron supports for acres of glass, with wood used virtually only in the floors, that Paxton, doodling on his table napkin in June 1850, modified to provide the answer to the committee's design problem.

Within three months, on the 26 September, the first cast iron pillar was erected and almost miraculously the completed Crystal

Palace, as the editor of Punch named it, was handed over in the following January to the delighted organisers and was ready to open its doors to the public on the 1 May, 1851. From inception to completion, incorporating 2300 cast-iron girders and 358 wrought iron trusses, took less than two years, a triumph for Paxton's design, the industry of the iron masters and builders and an illustration of what could be done without computer aided design, electrical power and nothing more than horse drawn transport to the site.

But it was the availability of rail travel that ensured the Great Exhibition's success. Six million visitors came to marvel at its exhibits during the 141 days it remained open to the public. Many came from the Midlands and the North, seizing the opportunity provided by the first excursion trains to see this spectacle in Hyde Park. Others came by coastal steamboats the total numbers being far in excess of those expected by the organisers, who were first concerned and then delighted at the overwhelming success of the project. The crowds, including the ladies in enormous crinolines, (magnificently coloured with the new dyes on exhibition) gazed in wonder at the brilliance of the palace, 63 metres long and 124 metres wide, its central arches rising up nearly 33 metres to accommodate within the building the tall elms that the locals had refused to have cut down.

The opening was spectacular. The Archbishop of Canterbury offered up a prayer that seemed to go on interminably and the choir of 600 voices sang lustily while the bass pipes of the great organ boomed out proclaiming the magnificence of industrialisation.

The floor space of over seven hectares housed an Aladdin's cave of delights. The Crystal Fountain, the epitome of the glass-workers' art, stood eight metres high and was made from four tons of pure glistening crystal glass. The Derbyshire block of coal, which had been delivered unbroken, weighed nearly twenty four and a half tons and an incredibly vulgar, if massive, sideboard was carved from a single oak tree.

The wonders of the world were laid out for the new travelling masses to enjoy. Belgian lace was alongside tapestries from France and emeralds, pearls and rubies from India, not yet part of the future empire. The products of the colonies were celebrated along with the sugar, tobacco, wheat and wool of the West Indies, Canada and Australia. Britain's own industrial growth was reflected

in huge steam engines, a giant 31 ton locomotive and a steam hammer capable of forging enormous beams. But the crowd-fetchers beloved by all the visitors were the Koh-i-nor (the mountain of light) diamond and an alluring graceful statue of a naked Greek slave girl. All are recorded in the massive three volume catalogue of exhibits that reflects the boldness and confidence of the Victorian community.

They read as a hymn to the ingenuity of the Victorians triumphing in the heyday of the Industrial Revolution, an almost reverent worship of the material. But if the contents were wondrous, if often grotesque, it was, in the end, the building, sublimely proportioned and glittering as the sun reflected from its multitude of glass facets, that over all caught the imagination of the visitors who continued to come in droves. Towards the closing days in October over 100,000 men, women and children, in a single day, crushed their way in determined to see this exhibition that pleased everyone. And it was here that London had its first public toilets which were so successful that 'spending a penny' brought in no less than £1,770!

So successful and well patronised had the building been that the profit of £186,000 was enough to finance its removal to Sydenham on the outskirts of London, where it gave a new name to the district, and allow Prince Albert to put in hand the erection of the Victoria and Albert and scientific museums in South Kensington. On its new site, the slightly enlarged building, was used for other exhibitions for over 80 years until it came to an ignominious end in 1936 when it was consumed in a spectacular fire. Its prototype, the greenhouse at Chatswoth, survived a little longer having to be destroyed by explosives after the Second World War.

The Koh-i-Nor diamond is now part of the crown jewels and many of the other exhibits remain in public and private collections but of the outstandingly triumphant great building nothing remains on the wind-swept site above Sydenham and a new generation perhaps doesn't know that a football team takes its name from the stroke of genius created by the pen of Sir Joseph Paxton.

Houses of God

Religious uniformity and dissent in Chesterfield

T HE UNOFFICIAL ECCLESIASTICAL CENSUS of 1851 tells us a lot about the religious institutions of Chesterfield at the time of the Great Exhibition. But the history of how the many dissenting groups developed in the town is also of interest.

The pattern in the Borough of the many churches and chapels had its roots in events two hundred years earlier when men of conscience struggling in an age of republicanism and its over-throw met in secret to foster their new-found beliefs.

Early amongst these were members of the Society of Friends, named from an event at Derby, the Quakers. Locally among their number was John Gratton of Bakewell who, after an experimental period, found himself at one with the Chesterfield Quakers. A member of the Society from 1668 to his death 43 years later he was a persuasive preacher often attending private houses in the town and neighbouring hamlets. For his pains he was betrayed by informers, planted by the Vicar, and fined £20 by Richard Clarke, the Mayor, despite Clarke having been at the service and having been strangely moved by Gratton's words.

Quakers were pursued even after the Restoration of Charles II and fifteen were incarcerated in the House of Correction in the Dog Kennels area, in 1663. Many were fined including so important a public figure as the lead merchant William Storrs who was fined the very large sum of £75. But despite such persecution the movement thrived, Fox, a founder, finding support in the town, and being joined by many leading tradesmen so that by 1689, when the Toleration Act became law, there were sufficient to warrant the registration of four meeting houses in Chesterfield.

By 1697 a committee of Friends had been assembled to oversee the building of a meeting house in Saltergate financed by a loan from Storrs. This simple, largely brick building, was rebuilt in 1770, with an internal gallery and was then hardly altered throughout its 150 year life until it was demolished to make way for the car park building in the 1960s.

Though some of the zeal declined after the first expansive years, their simple faith coupled with their practice of supporting charitable works, apprenticing young people and making loans to get people on their feet played a not insignificant part in the commercial and social life of the town. They took marriage seriously, approving and disapproving in a characteristic manner and their Chesterfield marriage records make interesting reading. It is there that the marriage of Mary Storrs to John Fry (whose son Joseph founded the chocolate manufacturers) is recorded.

But the Quakers were not alone in welcoming the Toleration Act. Large numbers of independent dissenters were without any place of worship and had to content themselves with secretive meetings in private houses.

Again following the Act of 1689, a prominent business man Cornelius Clarke, descendant of the first mayor, and now with a family seat at Norton, financed the purchase of land at Elder Yard to build a chapel to be shared by the Presbyterians and Congregationalists or Independents who had been more closely related in their belief until the Civil War. This building backed onto the closed land in what is now Elder Way and had its main entrance off Saltergate with a pedimented facade facing south only subsequently altered by the chancel bay on the east end.

Such a sharing arrangement lasted relatively amicably for thirty years being brought to a close only by the more intense movement towards Unitarianism at Elder Yard. The doctrinal conflict led to the transfer of the Congregationalists first to the Blue Meeting House (so named after its Welsh slate roof) in Froggart's Yard and then to their own Independent Chapel with its Tuscan entrance approached from the narrow Soresby Street, in 1822.

As with the Quakers, leading business men can be identified among the two congregations, men like Robert and Henry Malkin

Nonconformist Chapel,
Elder Yard

playing a role in fostering the growth of a Sunday School.

But in the year before the canal was opened which was to start the transformation of the industrial life of Chesterfield, a new spiritual force had made its initial impact. This was the preaching of John Wesley in the Market Place to a small gathering in the summer of 1776. The early days of Wesleyan Methodism within the Borough were not easy but after sharing room in Froggart's Yard and later in Packer's Row a sufficient strength had been assembled in the nineteen years after John Wesley's first visit to finance the building of the chapel on Saltergate and for its great extension in 1822.

Methodism had considerable appeal to the new industrial workers and the newly forming trade unions benefited from the discipline espoused by many of its leaders.

Other sects, Baptists and Arminian Methodists had premises in South Place, not far from the meeting place of the Independents, favoured by the successful draper Francis Hurst of Abercrombie Street, but it was to be some years before they built their own chapel (now a listed building) in Brewery Street. The Primitive Methodists, the so-called Ranters that had started up in Staffordshire, used a room in Chapel Yard, off Beetwell Street, and though they built their own chapels in Whittington and Brampton it was twenty years after that they founded a chapel in town. They were particularly committed to helping the poor and had outlier missions in Silk Yard and Brampton.

By the time the Ecclesiastical Census was taken many more dissenting sects were to be found with meeting places in the Borough. Primitive Methodists, numbered 375 on the census Sunday, and the Mormons, of the Church of the Latter Day Saints, who met in a room at the top of Soresby Street numbered 70. Near them the breakaway congregation of 300 Wesleyan Reformers had met since 1849.

And despite the increasing number of Roman Catholics in the Borough, a number swelling with the influx of Irish workers on the railways, the mines and the iron industry, no permanent meeting place was erected until three years after the census when the Church of the Annunciation, designed by Joseph Hansom (the Yorkshire architect responsible for the safety cab) was opened, a tower being added when it was extended in 1878.

Conflict between the established Anglican church and the Dissenting groups was bitter in many towns but this was not the case in Chesterfield, probably largely because of the temperament of Rev. Thomas Hill the vicar from 1822 until 1851, he is most popularly remembered for putting an end to the ringing of the church bells on the town's race days.

Throughout the early part of his incumbency there was growing concern that the Anglican church was losing membership to the dissenters and it was believed the provision of more seats would in part cure the unwelcome tendency. To this end St Thomas's was carved out as a new parish and a church built in Brampton in 1830 while another 1000 places were provided with the completion of Trinity Church in Newbold Lane and the chapel in the new Union Workhouse.

Despite these efforts, the modernisation by Gilbert Scott and the extended dedication of the spire church to St Mary and All Saints it is clear that what was missing was not seats but worshippers to fill them The census shows that 5823 places were provided for a population of 7101, Anglicans providing 2800, the Non-conformists

3023. On the census day 2798 Non-conformists took up their places but only 1761 Anglicans attended a service or Sunday school.

Reading between the lines it is clear that by the Great Exhibition Puritanical religious zeal was showing signs that it had lost its impetus but the importance of dissent among the new industrial workers was not to be underestimated.

Robert Watchorn

a little known benefactor of Alfreton

LFRETON HAS ONE OF THE MOST emotive of war memorials in the country. It depicts a Tommy, just reunited with his little daughter, as he thankfully returns home. It was erected in Alfreton largely because of the abiding generosity of Robert Watchorn.

The Watchorns hailed from Leicestershire, from where John Watchorn migrated to Ireland to try and better his lot. He made a good marriage to Alice Hogan, a staunch Roman Catholic, but was driven back to England by the economic ravages of the potato famine and settled as a miner in Alfreton. It was there in a small cottage, at No.2 Bacon's Yard, that they raised a family of seven children, the second of whom was Robert, born in 1859.

Robert was a bright boy showing promise at the school off Chesterfield Road but at eleven years of age he left to start work. He made a few false starts before being taken on at Swanwick colliery, where, for a shilling a day he sat in the dark for twelve hours opening and closing ventilation doors. But his thirst for knowledge and the chance to improve his lot spurred him to attend the evening classes run by the local solicitor, Ernest Bone, who thrilled him with stories of the opportunities awaiting young men in America.

On Sundays, since there was no Roman Catholic church in Alfreton, he attended St Martin's Parish Church but after a short while and a minor misunderstanding he directed his attention to the Primitive Methodist Chapel. Here he found inspiration and became a committed Methodist for the rest of his life.

His diligence led to improved work in the mine and a friendship with the Palmer-Morheads who owned Swanick colliery and with many other prominent Alfreton notables. By the time he was twenty one he had moved to Shirland colliery and was taking home a wage of 35/- a week but still felt he was not exploiting his potential to the full. In the following year, 1880, he made a momentous decision and emigrated to America financed from very meagre savings and a loan of £5 from solicitor Bone and £2 from the vicar.

In the States he joined a friend who had migrated a little earlier and was soon working in the mines of Pennslyvania before moving on to better paid work in the mines of Pittsburgh. This enabled him not only to send money home to help his brothers and sisters but also to pay off the loans. The local bank manager was so impressed by Robert's immediate achievements that he readily funded the cost of transporting Robert's parents and five siblings to America.

While his father found work in the pits Robert returned to England to attend an engineering course at Newcastle, entry to which had been arranged by Ernest Bone. But no sooner was Robert back in England than he had heard the catastrophic news that his father had been killed in a mining accident. Foregoing his course he returned to America and took up work as a miner and union official, being appointed in 1890 the first secretary-treasurer of the newly-formed United Mine Workers of America union.

It was early in this year that he attempted, with others, to rescue some thirty men trapped underground by a fire at the Dunbar mine in Pennslyvania. The attempt was a failure and the men remained entombed in a sealed off section of the colliery but Robert was awarded the gold medal of the Association of American Miners for his heroism.

In the following year he married Alma Simpson who remained his partner for the rest of his life and bore him two sons, young Robert and Emory. At the same time his life took a new direction when he was appointed Chief Inspector of Factories for his home state and engineered the passing of the Factory Inspection Act in 1893 which greatly enhanced the working conditions of women and children.

From this post he was head hunted, in 1905, to take on responsibility as Commissioner for Immigration at Ellis Island for a four year term. This was a period of great achievement for Robert

who was appalled at the squalor he discovered. By his efforts he changed the conditions under which poor migrants were treated beyond recognition installing a hospital and taking a personal interest in many whose condition was lamentable.

His posts as Chief Factory Inspector and then Commissioner brought him into contact with McKinley, whom he never got on with, Teddy Roosevelt and William Taft the President in 1908, who became great friends, so he was well acquainted when he left Ellis Island to join the oil industry. And it was in that industry, in which he worked for over thirty years, that he made his considerable fortune with the Watchorn Gas and Oil Company and the Alma Oil Company and established the town of Watchorn in Oaklahoma.

Wealth, however, did not bring unbounding happiness. His elder son, Robert, had died in infancy so that his elder boy Emory Ewart became the apple of his eye. Tragedy struck when Emory, an American Army pilot, was killed in a flying accident in 1921. As a memorial Robert donated much of his son's estate to a number of churches in California

It was at this time that Alfreton was struggling to find the money to erect its war memorial. Some funds had been raised but were insufficient and there might have been no memorial had not Robert Watchorn dug into his own pocket. Appropriately the memorial also bears the name of Emory.

This donation was to rekindle the long association Robert had enjoyed with Alfreton. He felt he wanted to put something back into the town of his childhood and in the 1920s remodelled the southern part. The old cottages of Bacon Yard and the Primitive Methodist Chapel building were swept away to be replaced by a magnificent new Methodist Chapel (to commemorate his Roman Catholic mother) linked to its own Manse and Sunday school. To ensure finance in the future he also built 34 houses to generate rent, making sure that those who had lost their cottages in the clearance had first choice at rents that did not rise in their life times and he set up the Robert Watchorn Trust.

Across the road, for the recreation of the townsfolk, he built a large park and to house his considerable archive of photographs of the passengers through Ellis Island, memorabilia and letters he built the Lincoln Library. Sadly this library was not used for its original purpose and was sold by the trustees to the local Masonic Lodge but much of the archives have been retained.

He died in 1944, just months before the SS Robert Watchorn was launched, but his memorials at Alfreton remain recalling a man of very humble birth who cared for his fellows and had an abiding sense of justice. It is not surprising that the War memorial at Alfreton is as emotive as it is.

Organic Chemist Extraordinaire

The story of Robert Robinson of Chesterfield

ALTHOUGH HE WAS one of the most outstanding sons of Chesterfield winning a Nobel prize for chemistry in 1947, being president of the Royal Society from 1945 to 1950, being knighted in 1939 and made a member of the Order of Merit in 1949 there is no memorial to him in his home town. No plaque marks his birth place or where he lived and if the Robinson Company muniment room did not proudly vaunt their family associate few would know of this exceptional man.

Robert Robinson was a charming boy born at Rufford Farm on the Baslow road out of Chesterfield, in September 1886. His parents were keen Congregationalists and made young Robert attend chapel regularly, which led him to a revulsion against all forms of organised religion throughout his life. But it was here under the guidance of the minister that he learned to play chess. The game fascinated him and, endowed as he was with a brilliant and restless mind, he became a noted amateur player and in later life wrote a book about the art of the game. He was also an accomplished piano player but was most at home hill climbing in the Peak and later abroad becoming a well known Alpinist tackling peaks on all the five continents.

He was the eldest of the five children born to William Bradbury and his second wife Jane Davenport. These five, together with the eight children surviving from William's first marriage provided a stimulating, if sometimes tumultuous, family circle.

Robert attended Mrs Wilkes, local kindergarten before going on to the junior school of Chesterfield Grammar. At twelve he was sent to the academically prestigious Moravian Fulneck school at Pudsey Greenside. His aptitude for sciences was readily recognised and though he wished to read mathematics his father who, had established the firm of surgical dressing manufacturers in Chesterfield, thought it would be more useful to the firm, which William wished him to join, if he studied chemistry.

In the event Robert never did join the firm but pursued a glittering academic career. His choice of Manchester for his first degree was inspired for at this time, 1902, the department at Manchester was paramount in the field of organic chemistry, the subject which Robert was to follow with an inspired passion throughout his life.

His interest in the chemistry of alkaloids as well as natural colours, and his first class honours led on to research which gained him his first doctorate in 1907 and a D.Sc three years later.

It was in that year, 1912, that he found time to marry a fellow student at the university, Gertrude Maud Walsh, who was to be a most supportive companion until her death in 1954.

From the start his output of scientific papers was prodigious, running to over 750 in his lifetime, and many universities wished him to join their staff. In 1913 he went to Australia to become Sydney University's first professor of Chemistry. Two years later he was awarded the Heath Harrison chair at Liverpool, going on to St. Andrews and back to his alma mater as professor before moving to London university in 1928.

At the beginning of the 1930s he was made a Fellow of Magdalen College and Waynflete professor of chemistry at Oxford until his retirement in the mid 1950s.

But his interests were not solely academic and he served both the British Dyestuffs Corporation and acted as an advisor to the Shell Research Company, while during World War II he made a notable contributions to knowledge of explosives and medicines, having worked on the study of penicillin and anti-malarial drugs.

His boyhood charm persisted throughout his life and he was always a good companion though he was often impatient with those holding views at odds with his own.

His research, which was hampered in later years by failing eyesight, led to countless academic honours and he received numerous medals from foreign scientific bodies, collecting no fewer than twenty-four honorary degrees. He was president of many learned societies but was most delighted at being made president of the British Chess Federation from 1950 to 1953. He died in London in February, 1975.

Surely one of Chesterfield's most outstanding progeny but remembered in the town more like Gray's 'village Hampen' as if he were some 'Youth of Fortune and to Fame unknown' rather than the town's perhaps most illustrious son.

Chesterfield's Schools

A little learning could be a dangerous thing

THE ROAD WAS SLIMY AND WET and the little girl hesitated at the doorway of the school, fearful of slipping as she tried to pass the cows herded into groups along the wall. She was one of the pupils of the new National School opened in 1815, off Soresby Street, a narrow lane shared with cattle on market days.

There had been schools in Chesterfield since the thirteenth century but they were for the sons of richer merchants. A grammar school had been founded, financed by the bequest of Sir Geoffrey Foljambe and confirmed by the 1598 charter, to fill the gap left after the dissolution of the monasteries and there were a host of dames' schools that came and went. But until the beginning of the nineteenth century there was no widely available schools to teach the three Rs to the youngest boys and girls of the town.

The land for the school in Soresby Street had formed part of the pleasure ground of Soresby Hall and had been purchased and given to the town by Joshua Jebb. Public subscription paid for the building.

Its declared aim contained nearly as many letters as there were pupils. It was 'the promotion of the Education of the Poor of the Town of Chesterfield in the principles of the Established Church upon the system originally practised by Dr Bell at Madras'. The furtherance of this intention was promoted initially by close links with the parish church but in 1845 allegiance was switched to Trinity church.

Promises made before the school opened were for a roll of around 400 and room was provided for that number but the number of pupils rarely exceeded 150, probably because even the few pence charged for attendance was beyond the means of many of the families of the town. And such attendance as there was fluctuated as opportunity for temporary work offered itself. Harvesting the potatoes saw a thin attendance and most of the boys were missing when, towards Christmastide, bulls were being baited in the bull ring, on High Street, before slaughter in the narrow lanes of the Shambles.

Despite the vagaries of attendance schools multiplied in number and by 1851 there were no fewer than 22 schools in the town, although the smallest two had only 19 pupils between them, and the largest was still the Soresby Street National.

Day schooling was, nevertheless, very much a luxury and the vast majority received what little formal education they had in the Sunday schools. It was there, with the Testament as the principal text, that children learned to read. And had it been possible to teach them to write without being able to read many would have preferred not to have been taught to read as it only filled young heads with alien ideas.

What to include in the narrow curriculum was always a bone of contention between the Anglicans and the non-conformists, and even though there were far more non-conformists than Anglicans, it was the latter who succeeded in dominating the educational scene.

But whoever won the argument the result seemed disappointing as the evidence taken in the 1841 enquiry into conditions in factories showed. The examiners found that very few of the 21 children, aged between eight and fourteen, employed in the potteries at Brampton, could read even though they had attended Sunday school regularly and some had also been to evening school and they labelled them as 'very ignorant'. Though this should hardly have been surprising considering the long hours children worked on six days of the week and makes the label seem very unfair.

Religion overshadowed education in the town and the Quaker, William Bingham, not to be outdone, sponsored a British school, close to his chandlery works in Hollis Lane. He followed the tenets of his religion strictly, refusing to pay income tax, preferring to

NEW FREE GRAMMAR SCHOOL, AT CHESTERFIELD.

have his goods regularly distrained, though he always bought them back!

For a long while there was no special provision for the children of the Irish population attracted by work building the railways and in the collieries, but a Catholic school was opened in the 1860s.

A further large National school, designed in the Elizabethan architectural style, was opened in 1845 on Vicar Lane. It was closely linked with the parish church, the vicar, at his own expense, providing fifty of the boys and fifty of the girls with blue coats with shiny brass buttons. Formally it was named the Victoria School to commemorate the visit by the Queen and Prince Albert to Chatsworth two years earlier but colloquially it was always the 'blue coats school'.

Teaching in all the schools was far from easy. All six classes of the 'blue coat' girls were taught at the same time in one room that was extremely stuffy and ill ventilated. Many of the children changed schools frequently as parents moved from job to job and lodging to lodging and rarely were more than 60 per cent of the 120 places for boys and 180 for girls filled.

By the year of the Great Exhibition, 1346 pupils were on the borough school registers, slightly more being boys than girls but there was still a pool of the very poor who slipped through the educational net.

To serve these most deprived children, who lived in the abysmal Dog Kennel slums close to the River Hipper, a Ragged School was opened in 1878. The initiators were mainly members of the Soresby Independent Chapel, including Henry and Arthur Slack, Herbert Shaw and Alderman Eastwood's family, who banded with others to found the much needed non-denominational school.

It opened as a Sunday school in the upstairs room of what had been an old factory and may in earlier days have been the old Waggon Inn. Places were available for 150 infants in the primary department and 250 pupils in the more advanced school.

So successful was it that it had to be rebuilt in 1914 (promptly being commandeered for military use for most of the First World War). For eight months the school had no home but alternative accommodation was found and the premises were regained in 1919 to serve the declining population as the slums were cleared away in the twenties and thirties.

After the First World War schools fit for the children of heroes were promised and by the 1930s the outdated Soresby Street School and the Blue Coat School, along with many others, had been closed. They were replaced by a new generation of buildings, Highfield Hall, Tapton House, Hasland Hall, Peter Webster's, William Rhodes and Violet Markham's girls school. It was these that ensured that no Chesterfield child need again be labelled 'as very ignorant'.

The Archbishop of Chesterfield

The Story of Archbishop Secker, who lived in Swines Green, now New Square

JUST AT THE TURN OF THE 17TH into the 18th century a small boy, just six years old, stood on Low Pavement at the top of Wheldon Lane, in the shadow of his half-sister's house. He was watching the other boys playing in the market square but kept apart because he was new to the town and did not know them. His name was Thomas Secker.

Far away in London another boy, the Duke of Gloucester, the last surviving child of Queen Anne and only a little older than Thomas, was soon to die and open up the succession to the Hanoverians. Young Thomas could not have guessed the eventual significance of this change, to him.

He had been born at Sibthorpe in Nottinghamshire, the second child of his young mother Abigail, who had become the third wife of his father, marrying him when he was nearly three times her age. His elder half-sister, Elizabeth, had married a very prosperous Chesterfield tanner, Richard Milne, and it was to this childless couple that Thomas was sent to live in 1699, just before his father died.

Whilst he must have missed his mother, her half-sister was pleased to have a child to care for and he was lucky to able to attend a local free school. The Milnes were non-conformists with a particularly puritanical bent and were worried that Thomas might associate with the less desirable characters who frequented the yards leading from the market square down to the River Hipper where

Richard Milne had his tanning pits.

To improve his environment Thomas' guardians, when he reached 15, sent him to Timothy Jolliffe's academy at Attercliffe. Jolliffe was a non-conformist minister who ostensibly taught the classics, but nothing corrupting like science or mathematics. The experience was not a success and Secker records in his autobiography that he forgot more than he learned and was pleased to leave after eighteen months at the school and rejoin the Milne's household.

He was unsettled. The taking of a degree at the old universities was not an option allowed to a dissenter and in the end Secker joined John Bowes, a fellow ex-pupil of Mr Jolliffe, staying at the Bowes' home in Bishopsgate, London.

These were young men of serious disposition and far from neglecting their studies taught themselves philosophy and joined the classes of John Eames to learn algebra, geometry and French.

Thomas seemed well on the road to fulfilling the wish of his father that he should become a non-conformist minister.

It was in this troubled period, however, that the serious minded Thomas started to have doubts about the theological foundations of non-conformity and decided it would be better to devote his life to another profession - medicine.

To this end he joined the eminent barber-surgeon William Cheselden, who was teaching anatomy in London, and gained practical experience of pharmacy with John Bakewell, a Cheapside apothecary.

To take his studies further Thomas went to Paris where surgeons had greater access to cadavers and were more able to practise dissections. It was here that he was introduced to the practice of man-midwifery, a branch of obstetrics which was, at that time, held in contempt.

Thomas did complete his studies, spending a short time at the University of Leydon where he was awarded a medical doctorate when he was 28. But then came the abrupt turn around in his career which would set him on the road to fame.

Following his conscience he felt called to abandon his non-conformity and enter the established church. After studying at Exeter College, Oxford he was ordained a priest in the Spring of 1723.

Promotion in the Church was rapid. His first appointment

was as chaplain to Bishop Talbot of Durham. Living in Houghton-le-Spring he soon endeared himself to the poor with his knowledge of medicine. His marriage led to his transfer to London for the sake of his wife's health and it was here that Thomas began his Hanoverian connection.

A sermon he preached at Bath led to his appointment as the Royal Chaplain and it was at St James' Chapel Royal that his sermon before the Queen led to an invitation to join Caroline's philosophic parties. So impressed was the Queen that she played a part in his election, in 1753, to the Bench of Bishops, albeit to the wretchedly endowed post as Bishop of Bristol, estimated to be worth £360 a year. Association with the royal house continued and two years later Secker was translated to Oxford where he was to play a role in trying to patch up the deep-seated quarrel between Frederick, the Prince of Wales, and George II.

Despite a brief period out of favour at Court, he was soon reconciled to the King and was elevated to the position of Dean of St Paul's in 1750. Thomas had baptised and confirmed George III so it was perhaps not surprising that eight years later he should be created Archbishop of Canterbury and go on to crown his sovereign and officiate at his marriage.

His new post was worth £700 a year, but in his sermons he

continued to deplore the failure of the Church and landed gentry to feed their hungry flock.

During his life he published a number of unspectacular learned works but is best remembered for his tall, impressive bearing and the earnest wisdom of his sermons. He retained a certain humility and when he died, in the summer of 1768, he was buried, at his request, in a remote passage of the cathedral at Canterbury without epitaph or memorial over his remains.

Thomas' half-sister had died when he was reading medicine in Paris and though he met Richard Milne from time to time he never came back to stay in Chesterfield. And how his avidly puritanical father would have viewed the rise of his son as a prelate of the established Church we shall never know.

The dissenting tradition remained in the Milne family, one descendant becoming a Presbyterian minister in Chesterfield, and medicine was practised by Richard's son, another Richard Milne, from the same premises at the top of Wheldon Lane where the young Thomas had stood so many years earlier weighing up his new playfellows.

A Soldier's Great War

letters from The Front

THE HALDANE REFORMS of 1908 saw the end of the old yeomanry volunteer battalions that had distinguished themselves in the Boer War and the creation, by an Act of Parliament, of new Territorial Battalions. This change-over was dramatically effected in Chesterfield at a grand ball held in the Drill Hall, then the Victoria barracks, when on 31st March, at the midnight hour, the Battalion Colonel Jackson enrolled as the first 'Territorial' of the newly formed 1/6th Battalion (Chesterfield). He was immediately followed by all his officers and men. Soon to join those officers was a young subaltern, Victor Robinson.

In the ensuing years Victor trained with his men, regularly attending the annual camps, and it was in early July 1914 at the Hunmanby camp in North Yorkshire that rumours of war started to circulate. On the 2nd August all training was suspended and the units were sent back to Derbyshire. War was declared two days later, all units were mobilised, and the 1/6th marched into Chesterfield to be accommodated in the drill hall and Central School. This sudden ending of peacetime soldiering was marked by the laying up of the Colours at St Mary's and All Saints, the parish church.

On the 10th August the battalion marched to the regimental depot at Derby, staying overnight at Ripley. Here they joined up with other Sherwood Foresters units in the 139th Brigade, before moving on to Luton and then Harpenden to commence the serious business of war training. By 15th November they were fully kitted out and standing by to be sent to join the B.E.F.

Lieutenant Victor wrote regularly to his mother and

fortunately some 60 of his letters and cards have been preserved. He survived some of the most bitter fighting and his letters, mostly short and many written in pencil by the light of a guttering candle, are reassurances that he is well but some give us a taste of what life was like for a young officer. One of the earliest letters was written just after Christmas Day 1914. Victor, aged 23, had been at a celebratory dance until the early hours of the morning when he received a message from the Duty Sergeant and was given an envelope marked 'Secret'. Inside was another envelope marked 'Open this in a room where you are alone'. The letter required him to report to the Brigade Headquarters some ten miles away. He set off immediately but his vehicle was involved in an accident and he didn't arrive until 6 a.m. His duty was to carry out a reconnaissance of the railway station and organise the en-trainment of the battalion. He spent the day at it and got back to his unit to find the operation had been cancelled!

King George V inspected the battalion, now part of the 46th Division, on 24th February, and five days later it set off for 'an unknown destination'. The crossing was made from Southampton and the 46th North Midlands Territorial Division made history by becoming the first wholly territorial division to join the B.E.F. in France.

More training ensued but by March 1915 Victor records his first experience in the trenches under fire: 'two bullets and six shells, but miles overhead'. The letter goes on more mundanely to say how much the officers relied on parcels from home. Throughout the war they had to provide all their own clothing and relied on parcels to break the monotony of issued rations. It is not then surprising that most letters contain thank-yous for parcels coupled with requests for gloves, socks, shirts, cigarettes and pipe tobacco. Finding something new to say without alarming his mother was clearly not easy but he was always looking for some small souvenir to send home that would give them a feel of his situation. One letter encloses a small fragment of Valenciennes lace he had seen an old woman making in the old way, not using a frame but plaited using 123 threads on bobbins.

The following month he wrote to his sister enclosing a small piece of barbed wire wrapped in a shred of sandbag. Victor had tried to find the bullet imbedded in a sandbag that 'had zipped between

Cpt. Victor Robinson,
MC, at Field House,
Chesterfield

me and the men I was talking to', to send but a half hour's search was of no avail. 'I am writing this,' he wrote, 'from a strong point made to be held if the trench is taken. It is a little sandbag fort built around a dug out. My bed is inside. During the day we sleep and feed and do carpenter work, during the night we work. Last night I pulled down one side and built it up again with better loopholes and extra buttresses. This is quite exciting work as you have to stand on top of the parapet most of the time and Gerboys keep sniping: they can see us when the flares go up but they can't aim at us so they just keep letting off lucky shots. We are quite a respectable distance off here, about 400 yards. Yesterday the artillery were very busy here, especially the Germans.........I've just been out to see what the Germans' artillery are doing today. Their first shell landed exactly 60 yards from here. It made an awful row but did no damage. They keep on about a shell a minute. That landed about 100 yards behind us. The next two have been well in front of us. I am in quite a decent sized funk as the next one ought by all the rules to land straight on us. That one didn't explode. I'll try and find it tonight. We can find the position of their guns from unexploded shells. They seem to have stopped for a bit. No they haven't. I'm trying to make up my mind whether to have jam or cheese for tea.'

The year was spent in and out of the trenches and Victor sent home some photos of the 1/6th Battalion and he encloses 'a cigarette case as a souvenir of a shell that landed near it: the same shell that killed Sgt. Woods. Can you send another, equally shell proof? I got buried and it gave me a great fright but no harm. I've just seen a German plane brought down; the first I've seen brought down. Six planes are up at present. All English. Soon after he writes 'We have just caught our first spy: he was signalling with a lamp to a Zepplin which bombed us'.

What he doesn't say was that this was a direct hit on a small block house occupied by Lieutenant Robinson and 19 other ranks of 'A'Company. Eight were killed and eight were wounded.

Preprinted field post cards follow where the sender deleted unwanted sentences and reassured those at home that the sender was well and had received letters or parcels. Then in November 1915, Victor, now a Captain, was 'mentioned in despatches' and was awarded his first Military Cross, the first in the Battalion. He was able to send home a copy of the signal which read 'General wishes to congratulate Captain V.O. Robinson on the award of a Military Cross.'

During the first winter the Sherwood Foresters had spent their rest periods away from the trenches in tents and Victor was not looking forward to a second very cold winter. Fortunately he writes in November that he is in a billet. Censorship made it difficult to say where he was stationed but in January, 1916 he was able to report the good news that his company was encamped in at a place overlooking the very blue sea where the city (Marseilles to which the Battalion had been withdrawn) was very damaged by the war and there were soldiers from Africa and India as well as English, Scots and Irish and German prisoners working on the docks.

This pleasant interlude was soon ended and Victor was back in Northern France. His Company was involved in an assault near Lievin and on April 1917 came a telegram saying 'Captain V.O.Robinson 6th Notts Derby Regiment was wounded on the 22 April 1917 but was able to continue duty'. This narrow shave and a lucky escape was followed in May by an even closer squeak when a shell killed the 2nd Lieutenant still behind him when Victor had just slid into a trench at the side of the road. In June he was awarded his second M.C.

Later in the year his letter records that the men had established a dairy herd and were feasting on the pigs and chickens that roamed between the trenches, a practice strictly frowned on but clearly presenting great sport. But more worrying was the plight of many dogs locked up and starving in houses that had been recently deserted.

In September Lt. Col. Vann took over the Battalion and Victor, now a major, became second-in-command.

By the start of 1918 the war seemed to be settling into a stalemate and the letters from Victor, written from Brigade H.Q to express mixed feelings that the Germans were done for, but then with a sense that they might make one more great effort. For a while he was in command of the battalion while Col. Vann was on leave. In August a number of changes were made and Victor was attached to the Eighth Battalion.

It was while he was with the 1/8th that the half expected

great effort came in the early Autumn. On 8th October he writes 'the 6th have been having a time. The Division has done two fierce attacks First against the Hindenburgh Line South of St. Quentin. The 6th crossed the canal and took hundreds of prisoners. Col. Vann was the first to reach the village and rushed the guns. 2500 prisoners taken by the Sherwood Foresters alone. Capt. Hipkins was killed going forward to Germans who had put up the white flag'. On the 17th October he wrote 'We have just been in for a fight. Perhaps you may have read about It so I thought I would let you know I am all right. This is the third big attack the Brigade has done without any rest and living in the open all the time. Everyone is fagged out. I started out without any weapons and ended with about six Boche revolvers and 40/50 Boche machine guns. Enclosed is the ribbon from an Iron Cross a German officer gave me I am all right'

It was this 'fight' that gained Col. Vann his posthumous V.C. and Major Victor won the second bar to his Military Cross. The long citation makes clear that it was his action at a critical moment that enabled his battalion to gain its final objective and his example and leadership that inspired the men with the greatest confidence.

As souvenirs he sent home, by a man going on leave, the sight from a 105 m.m. howitzer captured by the 6th at Lehaucourt on 29th Sept. when the 46th Brigade stormed the St. Quentin Canal and captured 7000 prisoners and 76 guns. He gave directions on how it should be mounted with a commemorative silver plaque

At the beginning of November he was ' engaged in fighting a weakened Boche. Engaged in rear guard action around Oppy' (near Neuvreuil) 'where Frenchmen were putting up flags while the 6th were still fighting in the streets.' But on the day of the armistice he was able to write , 'We have finished in a good place in a chateau not far from the Belgian border. For the last few days there has been practically no fighting and what there was nobody took seriously. It seems funny to think there will be no more shells or bullets but somehow I'm not as far as relieved as I expected to be ....I expect we will be home by next summer'.

For the last few months of his service in France Lt. Col Robinson commanded the Sixth, enjoyed some well earned leave in Paris and came back home to Chesterfield.

The recipient of three Military Crosses for bravery and

leadership he was soon back in place in his medical supplies and packaging company Robinsons of Chesterfield of which he became the very successful chairman.

Acknowledgement: *I wish to thank* Mr. Robert Robinson *for allowing me to publish extracts from his father's letters.*

Chesterfield's Youngest Chief Constable

Sir Percy Sillitoe K.B.E. - man of many facets

WHEN, IN THE EARLY SPRING OF 1923, Captain Percy Sillitoe strode into the police station at Chesterfield, as the newly appointed Chief Constable, there was no doubt in anyone's mind that a powerful captain of men had arrived to stamp his personality on the force. He was the youngest Chief Constable the borough had had and came with no previous British police experience, and Chesterfield might have missed him had not the Town Clerk accepted his late application for the job..

His father, an improvident Londoner, had three children of whom Percy, born in 1888, was the middle one, with a brother and younger sister. And because of his father's lack of resources his early education would have been rather sketchy had not his good singing voice won him a place at the strictly disciplined St. Paul's Choir School. When his voice broke he lost that place and although he had some private tuition at home after he was fourteen it was only sporadic.

At seventeen, through a chance meeting with a friend, his peripatetic career began with a short spell with an oil company, a stint as a trooper with the British South African Police in the old South Rhodesia and then a transfer to Northern Rhodesia where he was commissioned. It was here that he realised the importance of strict discipline, against which he had rebelled at school, and the value of a military chain of command battling, as he had to, against an exacting climate and a heavy work load. To his chagrin he contracted blackwater fever and he was forced to return to England to recuperate.

He soon recovered and it was on board the Gloucester Castle on his return journey from this sick leave that he met his future wife, Mary (Dollie) Watson, a Yorkshire lass to whom he became engaged in 1913. Their marriage was delayed by the War, Sillitoe serving in the skirmishes against the Germans in East Africa, but after he had a short spell as a political officer in Tanganyika they were able to marry.

Mary did not take to the rather artificial colonial life and after she also suffered a serious illness Sillitoe gave up his appointment and returned to an economically depressed Britain with no immediate prospect of employment.

He started to read for the bar but did not enjoy academic study and became increasingly depressed: a depression made deeper when, at his father-in-law's instigation he tried unsuccessfully for police posts at Nottingham and Hull.

But in 1923 his future prospects changed completely with his appointment to Chesterfield. Here, as in many of his subsequent appointments, his arrival was heralded as a breath of fresh air. Although the strictest of disciplinarians he was always fair and in consequence not unpopular with the officers and men he commanded. Always ready to support subordinates, he expected loyalty from them and left them to get on with their own jobs without interference from the top. Police officers he felt should rise, with experience, through the ranks and he had no time for theoretical educational institutions like Lord Trenchard's police college at Hendon. But he recognised the value of women in the force and recruited Jessy Webster, Chesterfield's first W.P.C. And he fought with incredible vigour to improve the resources available to the force, then in Chesterfield housed in the old court house, winning during his short stay, a new police station and fire engine, the fire service being part of his command.

By nature an ambitious man he saw that the Rotary movement would give him cachet and contacts with the most

influential men in the Borough and was pleased to get himself elected to the Chesterfield Club that had been formed shortly before his arrival.

Professionally his success in remodelling the Chesterfield police did not go unnoticed and within two years he had been tempted away to the East Riding force where, in a cause celebre, he supported a constable against the harassment of one of the local aristocracy. This enhanced his standing with his colleagues but made relationships with the local big-wigs more difficult and so it was with little regret that he moved again, this time as Chief Constable of Sheffield.

It was in the slums of that city, plagued by the vicious Mooney and Garvin gangs, that Sillitoe established his prowess as a senior policeman, organising two man flying squads that using 'reasonable force' quickly established an undreamed of tranquillity. It was here too that he pioneered the introduction of a forensic science laboratory, with Dr. Webster, later Professor of Forensic Medicine, whom he met during investigations relating to an horrendous physical attack on a woman in New Whittington.

The firmness of his command and his ability to up-hold the law against such odds commended him to the watch committee of Glasgow where, at forty-three, he took command of the city force, the largest outside London. In the ensuing twelve years as 'the big fellow' he cleaned up the criminal element, the Neds in the Billy Boy, Norman Conks, and Beehive gangs, before switching his services as Chief Constable to the Kent combined services brought together to co-operate with the military red-caps during the planning stages of the invasion of Europe.

Wisely, he contended, he had always been insistent that police officers should retire once they had qualified for a full pension to ensure young blood had its own opportunity and it was perhaps against his better judgement that he was persuaded to apply for the top job at MI5. Police service he thoroughly enjoyed but he took little pleasure from his work as the Head of this secretive commission. His period of service, running from 1946 to his retirement in 1953, coincided with the cold war defections of Guy Burgess and Donald MacLean and the unsavoury trials of Klaus Fuchs and Alan Nunn May. And, though his training and experience had been very varied, it had not prepared him for the flexibility required of Whitehall service and his presence was   probably resented by many of the quasi-mandarins who felt their own nominee should have got the appointment.

But despite this handicap Sillitoe executed his function with some distinction particularly helping with the setting up of the security services in those parts of the empire released to self-government.

When he died in 1962 his obituarists made much of his service at MI5 but Percy Sillitoe had been a man of many parts, living up to the family motto, 'Selito teneto si leto', (see it through) and his contribution of the policing of the Realm was outstanding. Chesterfield can count itself lucky that even for a short time he was able to put his personal stamp on our bobbies on the beat.

Chesterfield's History in Street Names

THE TANNERS AND POTTERS of medieval Chesterfield and its townships did a thriving trade and since both were big consumers of salt it's not surprising that the road leading west, to the wichs of Cheshire, was called the Salt Road. But because of the Scandinavian influence of the Danish invaders on the locals' speech they called the road the gata, now corrupted to gate, and so the northern boundary of the old town was called Saltergate that led into Ashgate, named after the family Ash (or Asche) that lived opposite Caus Farm.

The eastern boundary was the road to the lord's mill and the bridge across the Hipper was Souter Gate, the home of the shoemakers, until its name was changed to St. Mary's Street. Other old 'gates' in the town, like Gluman Gate, were most probably named after the glee-men who visited the town like Morris dancers and Knifesmith's Gate took its title from a family of that name who, it is most likely, in their turn gained it from their craft.

The yards, the survivors of the original burgess's plots, took their names from the most prominent resident tradesmen, such as Ward, Froggatt, Wheldon or Robinson, changing as traders came and went, while Spread Eagle Yard, and Peacock Yard reflected the names of the public houses standing in them. And Theatre Yard really had an active theatre in it right up to the middle of the nineteenth century. Across the market, Court 1, one of a number of courts, prosaically recalls huddled Victorian slum dwellings, too squalid even to warrant a personal name.

Beetwell Street may have been named after a family of that name but a betewell is also a brewing artifact so perhaps the well related to a chalybeate spring as did the reference in Spa Lane which led down to the Scarsdale Brewery, the road still graced with the gutter blocks to ease the passage of the horse drawn brewers' drays. Nearby Hollis Lane took its name from Holles, or Hollis, the family name of the Dukes of Newcastle who had properties in Bolsover, to which the lane led.

Another of the old families of Chesterfield is commemorated in Foljambe Road, recalling the Walton lord of the manor, thus expunging the reference probably to earthenware manufacture in its previous name, Pot Lane.

A more recent family is recalled by Malkin Street, no reference to grey cats or lewd women but named after the family of Tapton Lane that in the 1780s produced a mayor of the borough, had linen connections with Ireland and owned a sizeable estate taking in what is now Corporation Street, cut to access the railway station. Next door is Durrant Road named after the family who owned the verdant estate running down from what was the Royal Hospital to the river.

Linking these two is Brewery Road that led to the Chesterfield Brewery Company's property (now the site of the sweet factory), an example of the industries of the town being recalled by place names. Less obvious in this category are the Beaver Places in Brampton, and formerly off West Bars, that were the streets where the hatters worked, some no doubt made mad by the chemicals used in the process. And West Bars, the western boundary of the town, was one of the market toll bars.

The town's industrialists are recalled by Storrs Road, named after the seventeenth and eighteenth century Quaker family that made their fortune first as woollen merchants and then as canal carriers, and Markham Road recalling Charles Paxton Markham, the engineer who was such a benefactor of the town, his final gift being Tapton House, once the home of the railway pioneer remembered at Stephenson Place. And Clayton Street takes its name from the tannery. Wharf Lane, in Stonegravels, is where David Barnes had an iron foundry and loading bay beside the canal and Tap Lane, in

Brampton, commemorates the service utilities for it used to have one of the waterwork's standpipes to supply the local houses.

Other benefactors such as the Lords of the Manor, the Dukes of Devonshire, are recognised in Cavendish Street and Burlington Street, both open in the 1830s, a host of Devonshire Places and a Hartington Street in Spital, which takes its name from the medieval leper hospital. And even the Duke's agent, Soresby, is noted in the road running north from the market place, and the Manners of Haddon give rise to Rutland Road..

Few battles or wars are recalled. There is no Trafalgar Street or Waterloo Place though the Crimea war is recalled in Alma Street, in Brampton. The Boer war is, however, indirectly recognised via the generals at Redvers Buller Road, Baden Powell Road, and Lord Roberts Road between Boythorpe and St. Augustines, Lord Roberts having been made a freeman of the borough in 1898.

Three politicians get a mention: the Right Hon. James Abercrombie, Speaker of the House of Commons in the 1830s, who lived for a while at Stubbing Court, Cobden, the 1840s M.P. for the West Riding and William Ewart Gladstone, Victoria's long serving Chancellor and Prime Minister, the latter two having no apparent direct connection with the town. The old Queen Victoria is not remembered but Edward VII's son the Duke of Clarence and his Queen Alexandra, are.

The spirituality of the town is marked in Holywell Cross, St. Helen's Street, St. Mary's Gate, and most recently Church Way, and possibly Palmer's Gate, in the Shambles, for palmers were those who had made a pilgrimage to the Holy Land. Vicar Lane really was a narrow alley leading just to the back of the vicarage but Elder Yard does not refer to the patricians but rather to the elder trees that grew there.

Nearly as old as the elders' yard is the name Highfields derived from the days of open fields when the *great fields* were often

named from their location, while Brockwell Lane recalls more bucolic days when badgers were like urban foxes. Much newer is Jawbones Hill, on the road to Derby, so named because it once sported a giant-sized whale's jaw which might have marked where whale oil, used for lighting, was on sale.

In the heart of the town the Shambles, the medieval Fleshamols, where the butchers slaughtered their beasts, was once surrounded by lanes, laid out in gridiron pattern, and labelled by the trades they housed, Mercer Street, Potters' Row, Draper Row, Fisher Row, Iron Gate and Souter Row. Few now remain, but Packers' Row, at its edge, probably nostalgically recalls Chesterfield's medieval past when the wool packs brought by the jaggers' horse trains once journeyed down the Salt Road, through the town with the crooked spire.

The Genesis of the Staveley Coal and Iron Company

NOW THAT THE STAVELEY iron works has ceased to operate it is worthwhile looking back at how it developed in its earliest years.

Back in the early 1780s the Mather family of Nottingham, which had recently given up their lease of the Hunloke iron furnace, snatched the lease of the Staveley works from David Barnes, the tenant whom the landlord, the Duke of Devonshire, had found too un-enterprising. The French Wars were just about to clear away the depression that had followed the American War of Independence and there was a mini-boom in the demand for iron.

Walter Mather got the Staveley iron company back on its feet and made a reasonable profit up to his death in 1796 when continuity of the enterprise looked uncertain. Matters had been complicated by Mather's disinheritance of his only son and his bequest of the works to his two daughters. Their husbands, William Ward and Richard Lowe, were inadequate businessmen to take over control and the manager they appointed was so incompetent that he missed many of the opportunities the French War presented.

By 1810 the firm faced bankruptcy and was only temporarily buoyed up by loans from the Nottinghamshire banks of Wright and Wylde. But salvation came in a most unlikely way when Richard Lowe died and his widow married George H. Barrow a Southwell solicitor with no experience of iron making or heavy industry.

Ward's assessment of the continuing prospects for the firm

was so pessimistic that in 1811 he left leaving Barrow to nurse the company through the years of depression that ran right through the post Waterloo years and the 1820s

And this George Barrow did with surprising competence, for while he was no technical genius he was a competent administrator with a sound financial acumen. These were the traits that imbued the firm with stability and saw it safely, if somewhat precariously, through to the railway age, but with its future firmly underpinned by the hundred year lease George negotiated with the Duke of Devonshire in the doldrums years of the 1820s. It was this lease of coal bearing land which ensured the dichotomy of interests the enterprise would cultivate and which would carry it through to its outstanding importance by the turn of the century.

By 1840 G.H. Barrow was 61 years of age and ready to lay down the burden of running the Staveley iron company and was pleased to pass responsibility to his younger brother Richard.

For the previous 32 years Richard had been in partnership with his brother John and had built up a considerable wealth trading in the Far East and the Iberian peninsula. He had just retired, a bachelor of 53, when in 1840 George asked him to take over the Staveley Company. This challenge tempted Richard, a man, despite his Pickwickian appearance, of extraordinary drive and enterprise. Without hesitation he took over control of its labour force of 500 half of whom worked in the firm's coal mines, producing about 50,000 tons of coal a year, and the remainder in the iron stone mines and works turning out 5,000 tons of castings.

Richard recognised his technical limitations and brought in William Knighton as his manager, requiring him to rebuild the iron works to modern standards. But at the same time it was Richard, with his worldwide experience, who recognised the potential of the London coal market now that railways had cut the cost of access. So it was to the sinking of coal mines that he turned his immediate attention.

Within a year Speedwell pit, (reputedly named after one of his successful sea venture ships), was sunk and in production. Two years later in 1843 Hollingwood and Hopewell followed them and as capital became available Springwell was added in 1853 and the grand Seymour colliery in 1878. The Clay Cross Coal Company's hold on

London was broken and by the middle 1860s coal output had risen by fifteen times to over 700,000 tons a year helped by a new market for the manufacture of coke from small coal that was developed in Sunderland.

Nor was the ironworks neglected even though it was probably never as profitable as the coal business. Output quadrupled stimulated by the almost insatiable demand for iron for the railways and gas and sewage pipes.

While money to finance the enterprise was not at first a problem the scale of the activities was so vast that it strained even the resources of Richard who had in the end to borrow over half a million pounds from his brother John. No less a restraint was the problem of finding and keeping good labour.

This limitation beset all the coal and iron companies, Sheepbridge, Butterley, Clay Cross and to a lesser extent Renishaw. All attempted to solve the labour problem in the same paternalistic way by building houses, schools and chapels.

Only a relatively small fraction of Barrow's labour force came from around Staveley many hundred Irish immigrants living in Chesterfield and journeying to work by the 'Paddy mail', the statutory cheap daily train. To tempt men to join him, Richard had to build over 640 cottages, which by 1865, housed nearly 2000 work people, over two thirds of his total labour force.

The centrepiece of these developments was the model village close to Staveley named after the company owner, Barrowhill.The blocks of three cottages, built in local stone, were miles ahead of the hovels that the workers had shivered in fifty years earlier. With their large main room, small back kitchen, and three bedrooms and a shared privy in the yard they must have seemed like palaces, even when crowded with lodgers. Already they were an improvement on the first 175 Speedwell terraced cottages where the access to the bedroom, in some of the houses, was by ladder rather than stairs. But they were a far cry from Barrow's own mansion, Ringwood Hall, though to be fair he opened his gardens every Sunday so that his employees could enjoy them too. Perhaps he hoped it would make for more sober Sundays for absenteeism in the mines on Mondays and Tuesdays was an unremitting headache.

And Richard Barrow, like so many of the other ironmasters

and coal owners, recognised the need for an educated workforce, building church and national schools and meeting spiritual needs with non-conformist chapels and a fine institute as a leisure and educational centre.

He was a fair man who was much liked by his labour force, though some grumbled about truck when he deducted a shilling a week from each of them to finance a sick benefit club. But he could be a severe disciplinarian, not in the way that Stephenson was at Clay Cross with the strictest of rules about smoking and work place practices but still ready to flood a mine rather than allow the colliers to hold him to ransom by going on strike.

He was a forerunner of Charles Markham, who took over the management of the company in later years, having no time for trade unions, and in this way was unlike the later operators of the Sheepbridge Company.

The firm was by the mid-1860s once again running short of capital for expansion, and conversion to a limited company under the 1862 Act seemed a good way forward. With this in mind Richard Barrow sold out to a newly formed Staveley Coal & Iron Company, brokered by Chadwick from Manchester and the industrialists H.D.Pochin, Ben Whitworth and John Brown. Barrow remained as chairman but from now on the real power rested with Pochin and it perhaps was as well that Richard Barrow died in 1865 before he had completely let go of the reins.

Left behind was a sturdy competitor in what was to be a battlefield during the remainder of the century. George Barrow had nursed the ailing embryonic iron company and Richard brought it to vigorous manhood, its workers, better housed and educated to have relatively secure jobs..

Richard Arkwright the Younger

WHEN SIR RICHARD DIED in 1792 his only son, another Richard, took stock of his life and elected to change its principal direction.

Born in Bolton on the 19th. of December, 1755, he was brought up initially by his father, his mother, Patience Holt having died when he was only a few months old. Then when he was six his father re-married and Margaret Biggens became his step-mother.

Very little is known about his early life, and even less would have been discovered if hadn't been for the painstaking research of Bob Fitton. We do know that the elder Arkright had set up as a publican, the landlord of the Black Boy, but was still running the barber's shop across the road where he continued to make a reputation for himself as a skilled wig maker. At least, that is, until he was bitten by the cotton bug that caused him to devote the rest of his life to improving the spinning of cotton and in the process firmly establishing in Great Britain the factory system of manufacture.

By the time the young Richard was in his early teens his father had set up his cotton spinning mill at Cromford and moved to live at The Rock. And it was here the boy started to learn the intricate details of the trade and particularly the commercial niceties. Always by nature quiet he had inherited much of his father's head for business so that by the time he was in his mid-twenties he was sufficiently well breeched to buy from his father the Manchester mill in Millers' Lane. Here he entered into partnership with the Sampson brothers, who managed the business while Richard continued to live in his newly acquired house at Bakewell.

Despite the interuption of the American War of Independence, the long running cotton boom continued and by 1781 the young Richard, who had married Mary Simpson a year earlier, was ready to buy, again from his father, the corn mill bought at Rocester, on the Staffordshire border, which had promptly been converted to a spinning mill.. Here, with Richard Bidden of Bakewell, who held a third share in the enterprise, he continued to prove his managerial skills and in 1787 bought the site of the Cressbrook Mill, built by his father and recently destroyed by fire, from the heirs of Baker the land owner. At Cressbrook he re-employed William Newton (the Minstrel of the Peak) newly available after working on the Crescent at Buxton, to rebuild the mill and extend the housing for the pauper apprentices.

But he was not entirely happy just running factories and within three years of acquiring the Manchester mill he had sold out his interest to the Simpsons at a handsome profit, receiving over £20,000, paid in instalments over seven years and was thinking of other ways of deploying his rising fortune.

Meanwhile his father had also prospered and been knighted. He had generally enjoyed good health, apart from a troublesome disposition to asthma, but in his late fifties he started to show dropsical symptoms and despite the treatment by the eminent physican Erasmus Darwin of Ashbourne, he died in 1792. Much of his considerable estate was left by his will to the children of his second marriage, his many grandchildren and to charities but the more than modest but not overwhelming residue, including a number of the manufactures, passed to his only son Richard.

It was at this point that Richard, aged 37, took stock and decided to become far less dependent on the textile world to concentrate on landed property and banking. The mills at Nottingham, Wirksworth, Cressbrook and most of his own mills were sold, only the Masson and Cromford works, part of Bakewell and Rocester being retained.

The funds released by these sales were invested in the Government's Consolidated stock or ploughed into property. Before his father's death Richard already held £40,000 in the Funds and by the time of his death he had become the largest holder of the Funds in the kingdom.

He had little interest himself in the status significance of landed property, altough he did move first to The Rock and then

Willersley Castle, where he was intensely interested in developing the gardens throughout his life. But he did want to ensure his nine children enjoyed the privileges of the landed gentry and to ensure this end he had started by buying Darley Hall in 1790, followed by Skerne, near Driffield in Yorkshire, together with Skerne Hall Garth, two paper mills and a flour mill. This outlay was matched in 1796 by the purchase of Normanton Turville the Leicestershire home of the Tervil family with about a thousand acres of farmland which became the home of Richard III, his eldest son.

The acquisition of a small estate at Crich followed and then in 1809, after some hesitation and negotiation over the price, he bought from Lord Essex the Herefordshire estate of Hampton Court, for £230,000, as a home for his son John.

Ten fags and a twist

ATWIST AND A BOTTLE OF POP ON 278". Such was the demand from the diminutive collier's son at Langwith pit canteen. The Sheepbridge Company colliery, like the other Company pit at Glapwell, allowed credit to its employees the charges being made to the colliers' lamp numbers, to be knocked off their pay at the end of the fortnight.

The pop would have come from T.P.Wood's bottling factory in Knifesmith Gate and the marble to seal the top was as attractive as the pop in the bottle. The thick black twist would have come from Mason's tobacco factory.

Colliers were not allowed to smoke underground and sated their yearning for nicotine, and encouraged a good flow of spittle to counteract the swirling coal dust, by slicing off strips from the twist to make plugs of tobacco which they chewed endlessly.

George Mason, who was elected a Town Councillor in 1834, had, early in the century, established his tobacco works in Wheeldon Lane (named after the Wheldon family in the 1600s), that led down through the yard off Low Pavement and made its way to the bridge to Boythorpe. It was at the river end of Wheeldon Lane that Richard Milnes, who had cared for young Thomas Secker, had had his tannery in the days when the Hipper was crossed by stepping stones.

By the time George Mason started up his tobacco plant, the yard was a bustling sea of enterprises and people's houses but there was still space for Mason's horse to walk round a central pivot, in a tight circle, providing the motive power for the tobacco grinding mill. Industry was booming in Chesterfield and in the late 1830s the lane became even more crowded when Beardmore and Waterhouse shoe-horned their lace factory, complete with its steam engine and tall chimney, into the already packed yard.

Mason's tobacco, probably came to Chesterfield as the return load from Liverpool, replacing Brampton pots which were sent to the Mersey for export. In Wheeldon Lane it was sorted and graded. The fine leaves, chosen as fillers, binders, or wrappers, were rolled into cigars and the more damaged leaves of good quality were shredded into cigarettes while the discarded shreddings were ground down for snuff and manufacture into thick twist.

The trade supported three tobacco manufacturers in the borough in 1833 but by 1846 George Mason had captured the market and was the only one still in business, operating his mill in Wheeldon Lane and a retail outlet in New Square.

One of his two sons, Charles, joined him and the enterprise went from strength to strength. As the century wore on bigger premises were needed to meet the growing demand for cigarettes and the Masons turned their eyes to the old lace mill at Spital.

This fortress-like building, with a tall slim chimney alongside, stood some distance from the town in what was still a fairly rural setting. It had been worked from the 1830s as a silk mill by Smith Holmes & Co. and had been one of the industrial hopes of the town. Inside it was well lit with two rows of windows in opposite walls and when the owners gave evidence to the Commission on Children's Employment,in 1841, they emphasised how well the design of the building kept the employees of each sex apart each being provided with a separate row of privies. But despite the quality of the building the lace and thread trade had fallen on hard times and the mill was closed down.

It had stood in a considerable area of fields and was converted to the needs of a tobacco factory without too much difficulty. George Mason, now a wealthy man, moved into Spital House and when the Great Central and Lancashire, Derbyshire, and East Coast Railways were looking for space for sidings, the fields were sold along with Spital House. George Mason moved on to Eastwood House and his son, another Charles, joining him in the business.

The tobacco industry continued to thrive and the old building was extended as new machinery to manufacture cigarettes was installed. Hugh quantities of tobacco were imported direct from

Modern cigarette manufacture

the American plantations to be held in bond, duty paid, at Spital.

The firm, now trading as George Mason & Son, had established its reputation with a selection of proprietary brands which soon had one of the largest circulations certainly in the Midlands and probably through most of England and Wales.

Mason's Irish roll and pigtail twists, always good lines, became a particular speciality with an exceptionally wide sale. And by the turn of the century their popular Virginia brands like 'Golden Days' and 'Standard Gold' with their eye-catching distinctive packets could well have become as famous as 'Woodbines', 'Gold Flake' or 'Player's Navy Cut' and made Chesterfield rather than Nottingham and Bristol the centre of the country's tobacco trade.

John Player and W.D. and H.O. Wills, however, had other ideas and slowly the great British tobacco combines were established growing into the Imperial Tobacco Co. and the Chesterfield producer was squeezed out of the market.

Charles Lennox Mason sold out and retired to the south coast where he died in 1935 aged 74. The factory was closed and the building used by a cabinet maker and then by a joinery firm before being put to use by a tile and sanitary ware merchant.

Now Chesterfield is without this once important tobacco industry and there are no pits, let alone one at which a lad can order pop and fags, and put them on his dad's slate.

A Waste and Houling Wilderness

NOT UNTIL RECENTLY was travel either cheap or easy. Up to the 18th century travellers would have agreed with the intrepid traveller Celia Fiennes that the moorland west of Chesterfield was some of the wildest and most difficult country to pass through in the whole of England. She records the 'weayes were steep' and 'you were forced to have Guides as in all parts of Darbyshire'.

This view was echoed by Daniel Defoe on his travels when he described the road from Wirksworth to Matlock as over 'barren moors, in perpetual danger of slipping into coal-pits and lead mines' or having to 'ride miles together on the edge of a steep hill on slippery road, or loose stones' while he saw the moors as 'with neither hedge, house or tree but a waste and houling wilderness'.

The poor walked. Cattle, sheep, pigs and geese (their webbed feet coated in tar) were driven long distances on foot. Those who could afford it rode on the ubiquitous horse or journeyed more slowly on wain or dray. And strings of pack horses moved commercial loads. The wheels of the carts were narrow and cut deep ruts in the un-metalled roads, churning them in wet weather into impassable quagmires.

As the economy grew, from the end of the Commonwealth, traffic needed to travel further and as it grew in volume matters got worse. Parishes on through-routes suffered particularly as more and more long distance travellers passed through.

The way-wardens, appointed at random annually by the parish vestry meeting from among the parishioners, rarely had either knowledge or inclination to improve the quality of the highways which were the parishes' responsibility to maintain. A town like Chesterfield, in consequence, lacking a navigable river or any way to the sea until the canal was opened in 1776, was cut off from markets other than for valuable, light goods, like textiles.

Partial remedy came with the 'privatisation' of some of the main roads by the creation of turnpike trusts which at least in part transferred the burden of maintaining roads from the parish to the road users.

These trusts, formed by an Act of Parliament, were administered by trustees who had the power to appoint their own successors. The trustees were often local industrialists and landlords who wished to improve a particular stretch of road in which they had an interest.

In exchange for improving and maintaining roads the trustees were empowered to levy a toll from the road user, often simplifying this task by auctioning their rights each year to the highest bidder. Technical responsibility was given to the professional turnpike surveyors, who still retained some rights to call on the parish for labour under the older statute.

One of the earliest turnpikes in Derbyshire was intended to be the road from Worksop, via Chesterfield, to Bakewell. The Worksop to Chesterfield road was improved and gated, or chained, in 1739 but the Chesterfield to Bakewell section was not turnpiked for another twenty years. A short section from Bakewell across the moors to Chesterfield, started in 1739, was soon abandoned. The road from Sheffield through Chesterfield to Belper was tackled in 1756 and the way to Matlock four years later. Further turnpikes followed quickly and by 1820 the whole county was criss-crossed by 49 main turnpikes and feeders like Birkin Lane outside Chesterfield.

Birkin Lane is still so named where it passes through Temple Normanton to Grassmoor and through much of the parish of Wingerworth. The turnpike was created by an Act with a title nearly as long as this second longest lane in England, "the road from Mansfield and Chesterfield turnpike road near the nine milestone from Mansfield through Temple Normanton, Tupton New Inclosure

Matlock Bath, typical of inaccessible
Derbyshire in the mid-1800s

and Birkin Lane to Buntingfield Nook in the parish of Ashover in the County of Derby".

Distances along the toll roads had to be marked by milestones and some of these remain, though road widening has destroyed the majority.

The tolls were collected at the toll houses which manned the barriers across the road. The gates have all disappeared but the toll houses can be identified by their closeness to the road and the little double faceted windows that gave a good view of approaching traffic up and down the road.

Most tolls were levied in cash, though regular users could pay a lump sum at the beginning of the year and get a rebate for under use. The collectors, wisely, deducted their wages before paying over collections to the Trustees.

On the Birkin Lane turnpike a coach, chaise, calash, chase-marine, or hearse, drawn by six horses or other beasts, paid one shilling and sixpence, the equivalent today of about £4. The toll fell to one shilling if only four horses were used and two horses brought the fee down to sixpence while a one-horse chaise was charged threepence. A score of cattle could pass for ten pence and the same number of sheep or swine for five pence. To suit the interests of the sponsoring trustees many commodities like lime and coke were exempt from toll as were dung and compost for gardens and land, ploughs, harrows and instruments of husbandry.

Although some turnpikes paid trustees handsome dividends many did not. The takings on the Birkin Lane pike were only £104:15:8 for the whole of 1774 (equal to about £5,400 in current purchasing power) so little was available to pay for maintenance or to redeem the mortgage of future tolls used as the initial finance.

Even though the turnpikes had made travelling more reliable and comfortable they did not cut the cost a great deal and coach travel was still for the wealthy rather than the common man.

Cheapness came with the railways which rang the death knell of the turnpikes. Mere feeders like Birkin Lane by 1876 only had a toll income of £33:6:6 but still carried mortgage debts of £1030:15s 7d. By the end of the century the County Authorities were taking over responsibilities for the road system constructing roads fit for Austins and Morrises. And the roads that had been impassable because of their inadequate construction are today, two hundred years on, so gridlocked by motor-traffic that the case for levying tolls is again being debated.

Violet Markham C.H.

A stateswoman and benefactress of Chesterfield

AMONGST THE MAYORS OF CHESTERFIELD perhaps the most remarkable have been the lady mayors and of these the first lady mayor, Violet Rosa Markham, is clearly the most outstanding not only for her work in the Borough but also as a national figure.

She was born at Tapton House in September 1872, the fifth child of Charles Markham and his wife Rosa Paxton. Her siblings, three brothers, Birdie, Arthur and Charlie, and a sister, were several years older and Rosa was not over pleased at the arrival of a new baby . Her father was even less impressed, recording in his diary his greater interest in "shooting 31 and 1/2 brace of grouse and birth of 2nd daughter."

Her childhood spent at Tapton was a happy one. She discussed politics, Home Rule for Ireland and the Boer War, with her father the Managing Director of the Staveley Coal and Iron Company, who sadly died when she was fifteen . And from her mother Rosa she learned how to run a large household when their family of seven had a staff of eight and became imbued with her mother's doctrine, 'The more I give the more I have.'

Her French governess taught her to speak French fluently and as the academic member of the family she enjoyed her time at West Heath School near Richmond, where discipline was sensible and not coercive.

In 1899, as war loomed inevitably in South Africa, she visited there and met Sir Alfred Milner and many of the political leaders. She supported the British cause and was very ready to argue her case strongly. It was here too that she fell under the influence of Arnold Toynbee.

The end of the Victorian era was not one of 'good old days' for a large proportion of the country's populace. Poverty was rife. Slum housing was all too common and appalling. Sanitation was still incredibly primitive. It was Toynbee who finally opened Violets eyes to these evils and, being a Markham, she determined to do something about it.

The Settlement Movement was starting up across the country and Violet Markham, now made independent by the gift to her of a considerable fortune by a friend of her father's, put her own money into leasing a property in Church Lane to start the Chesterfield Settlement.   Its prime purpose was to offer an opportunity to the poor who had missed the opportunity of a formal education, to provide opportunities for deprived women and their young families to be given a sense of purpose.

With the advice of Mary Tennant and ably assisted by Hilda Cashmore and Elsie Wright, Violet Markham soon had a mothers' medical clinic and school for mothers operating; a service that continued for 55 years until the responsibility was taken over by the Welfare State. So successful was the Settlement that it had soon extended its cover to deal with the need of mentally and physically handicapped children. Before this they had simply been neglected but the Settlement provided an opportunity to develop each child to its fullest potential. By 1932 27 such children were being taught, a service that continued at the Settlement until the Local Authority took over the responsibility in 1937.

To satisfy the adventurous spirit of youth she personally funded a base at Darley Dale so that youngsters could go on expeditions; the forerunner of the Duke of Edinburgh's Award scheme.

This interest that Miss Markham had in education had been harnessed initially in 1897 when aged 25 she had joined the Chesterfield School Board set up under the Elementary Education Act of 1870. This Board was empowered to levy a rate, deal with the

burning question of the day, the teaching of religion in schools, and build and maintain schools, raising the necessary funds. She made an impression on this Board and when it was wound up in 1903 she was at once co-opted to the new Chesterfield Education Committee.

Despite her commitment in the years ahead to a great deal of national work she always remembered the needs of Chesterfield. She played an important role in the building of six new schools and the improvement of many others during the early 1930s so that Chesterfield moved up from being one of the least well equipped boroughs to being well ahead in the educational field of many very much larger and wealthier towns.

Adult education was one of her main concerns. It was neglected in Chesterfield and Violet took great pains to restart the Municipal Technical Instruction Courses in the evenings. Written work was not popular with the participants so she introduced at her own expense a scholarship scheme to reward the student producing the best written essay in the year.

Politics had always interested her. She had seen her father's defeat at the elections when she was 14, had helped her brother Arthur at the famous Roseberry meeting in Chesterfield in 1901 to stimulate the flagging Liberal party (not much of a success) and had played an important role in his successful winning of the Mansfield seat. After his death in 1916 Violet Markham was one of the few women to stand after the War in the Parliamentary election. She was trying for Arthur's old Liberal Mansfield seat but was roundly defeated.

Surprisingly, though a feminist, she was initially actively opposed to Women's Suffrage at the early part of the century. Only after the Great War had shown her what an important role women could play in the life of the nation was she converted to the women's cause.

But it was local politics that she wished particularly to foster being opposed to the insidious moves already afoot to centralise governmental control. She was elected to the Borough Council in 1925 and was made Mayor for the year 1927/28. This brought her ex officio on to the Education Committee, becoming its chairman in 1929 until she retired in 1934 when most of her outstanding educational work had been completed.

While she had been in South Africa on one of her visits, (she was for the a
ge a much travelled lady, visiting Canada and China and Japan via the Trans-Siberian Railway) she met Major James Carruthers who was on the Governor General's staff. They were married in August 1915. He survived the War and they spent much of their married life based in Gower Street, London, apart from a period in Germany with her husband, where she painfully learned German. He died in 1936.

She had a strong low church Anglican faith and successfully led a group of parishioners who opposed the intention of the Rev Dilworth Harrison to make far-reaching alterations to the inside of the St. Mary's and All Saints parish church.

And though she did all this work in Chesterfield she still found time to write four well received books and serve with great distinction on the two Boards of Enquiry into conditions for women in the armed services in two wars. An executive member of the national Unemployment Assistance Board and its successor the Assistance Board (that slowly took over the responsibilities of the old Poor Law) she also served on the Appeals against Internment Tribunal during the Second World War.

Among the first creations of the Order, she was made a Companion of Honour in 1917 and was awarded honorary doctorates by Sheffield and Edinburgh universities. In 1952 Chesterfield made her the first female Freeman of the Borough. Her memorable life ended in 1959.

A Chesterfield school and a Probus Club used to bear her name and were reminders to all of this remarkable daughter of Chesterfield who now may, all too soon, be almost forgotten.

We are the soldiers of the Queen, my Lads

Chesterfield's Military Connections

I N NO WAY could Chesterfield be thought of as a military town. It has no castle or barracks though its name does derive from the presence of a Roman fort and its earliest military connection would have been with the legions in the latter part of the first century.

Its next brush with militarism seems to have been the so-called battle of Chesterfield in 1266 when Robert de Ferrers, the last Earl of Derby from that family, with support from Baldwin Wake and Henry de Almaine rose against the King. He was captured in the parish church and was hauled off to the Tower suffering the confiscation of all his lands.

The Civil War left the Borough fairly untouched though the parish church was seriously vandalised by the Parliamentary forces of Thomas Gell, Sir Thomas Fairfax and Thomas Hallowes assembled to skirmish near Calow with the Earl of Newcastle's supporters of the King.

Peace prevailed in the town until an ugly incident in 1805. It arose when men of the 2nd. Battalion of the 59th Regiment of Foot, the Nottingham Regiment, were billeted in the town. A drummer lad was sentenced by court martial to be flogged with the cat-o'-nine tails for striking a sergeant. Such military penalties were not then unusual and their severity, perhaps as many as 50 lashes, was horrendous.

On the day of the punishment the troops assembled, in

hollow square formation, on the parade ground at the St. Mary's Gate end of Beetwell Street and the usual large crowd of town's folk gathered to watch. As the lash continued to fall, flaying the flesh from the lad's back, the crowd grew restive and soon stones were being thrown at the troops and their officers.

As soon as the punishment was over the commanding officer, Major MacGregor, with his fellow officers, withdrew to their house near the market square. The crowd followed and spurred on by Joshua Batty, a shoemaker, they ripped up cobbles and broke every window and seriously damaged the roof. MacGregor waited inside for the civil authority to request his help in restoring peace but taking no other action. Only after some hours did the Mayor make such a plea and the order was given to beat the call to arms. This was done for three-quarters of an hour but the troops, who had stood around playing no part in the riot, refused to fall in and it was only the persuasive powers of the brave Mayor, as Chief Magistrate, that finally led to the mob moving away.

This was a serious breach of military discipline which was reported to the War Office. After much bureaucratic to-ing and fro-ing Batty was indicted at Derby Assizes for provoking a riot. Unfortunately there is no trace of how he was dealt with at his trial but the regiment was moved on to Ashbourne.

This 2nd Battalion of the 59th had been raised in Chesterfield in 1804 and included a number of local men. It saw service in the Peninsular war fighting out from the base at Corunna and acquitting itself very courageously collecting a series of battle honours. Three Chesterfield veterans of that war, Messrs Swift, Simpson and Glossop, supervised the firing of four six-pounders in a royal salute when Queen Victoria visited the town in 1843.

At the same time as the Nottingham Regiment was stationed in town the Chesterfield Volunteers, formed in September 1803, were being mustered as part of the precautions stemming from a threatened invasion by Napoleon. The force under the command of Lt. Col. Gladwin (the son of General Gladwin), supported by Lt. Col. Jebb and Major Waller, consisted of four companies, each of between eighty and ninety men commanded by Captains Bernard Lucas, Joseph Gratton, Thomas Bower and John Charge. The local Lucas company officered by Lieuts. Hinde and Wragg and Ensign

THE SHERWOOD
FORESTERS.

Sergeant.

Wilkinson had the Rev. Ralph Heathcote as Chaplain and the man-midwife and surgeon John Cartledge as medical officer. Their parade ground was in Beetwell Strret and they performed manoeuvres on Brewery Field near the Canal Wharf, which was later occupied by the Great Central Railway station.

Col. Jebb had served in Jamaica and the black servant he had brought back and who married into the local community caused quite a stir. Several other local dignitaries served with the volunteers including John Barnes of Ashgate (whose uniform is still in Nottingham Museum). They camped at Deal but were never put to the ultimate test the force being disbanded in 1829.

Apart from a couple of incidents involving Irish excavators, labourers living in Chesterfield during the building of the railways, the town seems to have followed a peaceful course. The first incident was in 1838 when a contingent of Nottingham Hussars arrived in the town to keep the peace. The local magistrates denied they were needed but by later agreement they stayed for a considerable time to ensure the peace was maintained.

The second came to be known as the Baron de Camin affair. Again the 'navvies' were involved. In the summer of 1862 the baron, who was rabidly anti-papist, planned to lecture on this theme in the assembly rooms in the market hall. The town had been liberally flyposted and the titles of his proposed talks incensed the Irish members of the community. After an unsuccessful attempt to speak the baron was warned by the Superintendent of police that he should not make a repeat attempt. Ignoring the warning, and proclaiming the right of free speech, the baron announced he would lecture. This announcement inflamed the already tense situation and near riotous behaviour ensued. The Mounted Volunteer Rifles were at drill in Beetwell Street and they claim they were asked to stand by and so came under the Mayor's control. As the troubles increased Lieut. John Brown, of Rose Hill, who was that day commanding the local militia, fearing that serious injury might occur decided to act to quell the disturbance. On his own initiative, dressed in his black 'crow' uniform, he ordered his mounted men to draw their swords and drive the crowd out of the square. His action led to the clearance of the market place but some women and children got jostled. In a subsequent enquiry the Mayor denied he had ever requested military aid and Brown was severely reprimanded for his action undertaken without the proper authority of the magistrates. Nevertheless his sword became a treasured family relic.

This second incident involved the re-formed Volunteer Rifles that had been recruited in 1859, after the Crimea War. The war abroad and the disturbances of the Chartist Riots at home had persuaded the War Office once again to sound a call to arms. It was with war engendered patriotism that the Mayor and a posse of town worthies engineered the reformation of the Chesterfield Corps, digging deep in their pockets to purchase the necessary equipment.

Among its members were T.P.Wood, Alfred Barnes, J.S.Rooth, and Henry Osborne. Commanding the battalion (which also had a unit at Clay Cross) was Major Hallewell, with Captain J.B.White in charge of the local Corps. Camps were held annually and the Corps was represented at the great Royal Jubilee Review at Windsor, travelling down on the day and only just getting on parade with ten minutes to spare.

During the Boer War six members of the Volunteers served in South Africa with the Second Volunteer Active Service Company of the Sherwood Foresters, where one of them, a Lance Corporal T.P.Margereson, died of disease. While they were stationed at Swartz Kop, near Potchenfstroom, they threw up a protective sand mound with 'Chatsworth House' surmounted by a buck picked out in white spa on the front. Proclaimed heroes, their homecoming in the S.S. Canada in 1902 was a great local event. Held up by fog in the Channel their arrival in Chesterfield at midnight was missed by the crowds that had turned out on the two previous evenings. But on the day following their safe return they marched through cheering crowds, with the Temperance Band playing *The Soldiers of the Queen*, from Brampton to the Market Square where the Mayor met them and took them to a sumptuous dinner.

In the early years of the twentieth century the Territorial Army was formed. Local men joined for the fellowship and the summer camps but they were rudely awakened when they were drafted in 1914 to the First British Expeditionary Force. They were joined by ardent comrades, many only young lads like the drummer of the 59th and like him they suffered cruelly.

Water water everywhere

but only a drop to drink: the story of Chesterfield's water supply

F EW CESTERFELDIANS would know where Tap Lane is and probably fewer why it got its name.

Back in the seventeenth and eighteenth centuries the towns-folk of Chesterfield drew their water from the Hipper and Rother as their forebears had done to supply their need for dyeing and tanning. And for drinking, the 5,000 souls in the borough relied on wells sunk in their yards and gardens, though many were happier to use alcohol to kill off the bugs and drink beer (for which Chesterfield had a good reputation).

The market place pump, rebuilt in 1825, drew its supply from a deep borehole and dispensed potable water but by the beginning of the nineteenth century, as the town's population grew, such pumped supply could not keep pace with the demand for clean water.

The first serious attempt to increase supply was taken that same year when the Chesterfield Waterworks and Gas Light Company was formed by private act of Parliament. This had been initiated by a public spirited group of business men, led by the Stonegravels engineer John Gratton, with the intention of 'improving and protecting the lives and property of the inhabitants by the provision of a pipe-borne water supply'.

The intention was good but the new supply, fed by gravity

through cast iron and earthenware pipes from a weir across the Holme Brook, on the Donkey Racecourse, near Woodnook Lane was not an over-night triumph. The water was stored in a 75 foot diameter reservoir at West Street and was untreated in any way and was often uninvitingly cloudy and occasionally had a most unpleasant smell. Not surprisingly it was much criticised, contemporaries saying it was so murky that, 'the poor used it as soup, the middle class only for washing their clothes and the elite for watering their gardens'. But the Brampton potters made a killing, seizing the opportunity to do a brisk trade in pottery water filters.

Water borne diseases were rife in many places the sewerage system being extremely primitive and always likely to contaminate underground water courses. Derby city suffered seriously from an outbreak of cholera, pollution showing no respect for birth or breeding and even Prince Albert meeting his untimely death from the lethal effects of such contamination. But Chesterfield was fortunate and despite the lack of treatment no water borne epidemic is recorded in the town.

The piped supply was only delivered to selected houses the majority of the populace having to rely on tap outlets in the streets that were shared by many households. Water was drawn and carried home in pails and tin-jacks or bought from water carts and although the quantity supplied was equal to ten gallons a head each day, the actual usage varied very considerably from house-hold to house-hold.

As Chesterfield industrialised the demand for water grew and forty years after the first water company had been formed a new one was registered to take supplies not only to Chesterfield but also to the townships of Brampton, Newbold,Walton, Tapton and Hasland. To meet the enhanced demand of the 16,000 people in these communities the company was granted statutory powers to build the first 31 million gallons reservoir at the lower end of the Linacre valley. This delivered water through a new nine inches diameter main to service a reservoir at Club Mill, enlarged to hold three million gallons.

Almost before the reservoir was brought into use it was clear the town was growing so fast that an even larger reserve would be needed and in 1865 the 126 million, top Linacre reservoir was commissioned and the supply area extended to include Brimington, Calow and Whittington.

As the century wore on the company became less efficient and there were clashes with the Corporation, dissatisfied with the service the Company was giving. Leakage from the supply mains had become a serious problem which was not tackled until 1895, after some particularly serious drought years, when a new public company, the Chesterfield Gas and Water Board was formed. Very quickly the new officials set to, metering the net-work, cutting the wastage by half and petitioning for the construction of a third, (middle) reservoir 42 foot deep, with a capacity of 90 million gallons. This was built in 1904 when an effective filtration and chlorination system was introduced.

And still the demand for water grew as the town expanded. Thought was given to putting a tunnel through to the Baslow catchment area to feed into the Linacre reservoirs and pumping from the River Hipper was considered. But no decisions had been finalised when the First World War interrupted all such planning.

By 1920 the time for indecision was past and the increase in demand was met by sinking a borehole to the particularly sweet water at Whispering Well (which earlier had supplied Manlove's Holymoorside factory) and at Hunger Hill, both of which have given supplies of exceptional quality. They were only just sunk in time, the following year suffering an exceptional drought.

As houses 'fit for heroes' were built after the First World War more and more were provided with an individual water supply so that by the time the gas and water functions of the Board were divided in the early 1920s average consumption had doubled over the century and 50 per cent of houses had water-borne sanitation and 15 per cent had baths.

The responsibility for water supply had passed to Chesterfield Corporation in 1920 and in 1933 it joined with Bolsover Corporation to form the Chesterfield and Bolsover Water Board bringing into local service a million gallons of water daily from the Whaley Well water scheme.

But still the demand for potable and industrial water grew. In moves to improve efficiency and rationalise supplies the Government became increasingly involved. Locally this led to the establishment of a larger Chesterfield, Bolsover and Clowne Water Board and then in 1963 the North Derbyshire Water Board was formed to service an area extending from Buxton to Clay Cross.

Today the Severn Trent Water Company is responsible for the area's water supply and provides over 50 gallons per head daily, drawing supplies from the River Derwent and holding reserves at Ogston and Carsington.

The Linacre reservoirs are now no longer an essential part of the area's supply but provide a peaceful setting for leisure activity.

And Tap Lane? Now just a short cut from Chester Street to Wheatbridge to avoid the West Bars roundabout and not a sign of a tap, or the sound of the cry 'Two buckets for a ha'penny'.

The Busy Bees of South Street

HIGH UP ON THE ROOF LINE of the buildings at the south end of South Street is a mysterious tablet whose presence no one can account for. For perhaps a hundred years it faced the road, but was placed upside down so that few recognised that it was emblazoned with the arms of some important person.

When Britts, the ironmonger's shop, was being refurbished in 1989 the tablet was recognised for what it is and it was restored the right way up. It depicts, around a chevron, three bees and has been identified as the arms of Sir Richard Westmacott.

Sir Richard's father, who was also a Richard, had established a reputation as a sculptor, and especially as a designer of the then very fashionable ornate chimney pieces. Richard senior was anxious that his eldest son should follow him in his art and in addition to giving him his first instruction sent him to Rome in 1793 to study under Canova.

His exceptional talent was apparent from the start and within two years of his arrival in Rome, aged 18, he was awarded the Pope's gold medal for a superb bas-relief of Joseph and his brothers.

But these were troublesome times in Italy and as the French army approached Rome Richard travelled north through Bologna and Venice, crossing the Alps to Germany and arriving back in England late in 1797.

He immediately made a mark in London exhibiting that year and in almost every one of the next 42 years at the Royal Academy. His popularity with the rich London and provincial clientele never wavered. Initially he specialised in busts and had a following almost as large as that of Chantrey - another Derbyshire artist and sculptor.

His fame spread and works were commissioned from the colonies and the Raj in India.

At 36 he was elected a full member of the Royal Academy and his services were much sought after by those keen to be remembered by posterity through their effigies in chiselled marble. From his studios in London he produced an endless series of brilliant funeral memorials that are still to be seen throughout the churches of the land.

The Mary Chichester memorial at All Saints, Derby, the George Brittle at St. Peter's Belper and the three Pares memorials at Ockbridge are local examples of his work.

Nearer Chesterfield is the chimney piece at Chatsworth by Westmacott and Sievier and a delightful statue of Mary, Queen of Scots, tucked round the back of Hardwick Hall.

He was professor of Sculpture at the Royal Academy and lectured there to within two years of his death in 1856. But it was his public works statues, the bronze Achilles in Hyde Park, the equestrian George III at Liverpool and the panels on the Marble Arch (then in its original position outside Buckingham Palace) that ensured his knighthood bestowed in 1837.

It was then that he was granted the armorial insignia depicted in South Street and blazoned as : 'gules a chevron cotised argent between three bees volant and a chief or' surmounted by a crest (which is missing from the South Street tablet and may have been broken off) 'on a mount a column of the Tuscan order fesseways thereon a bee all proper'.

The carving is of a high quality and may well have been prepared for a tomb or to enhance a noble residence. If so why ever did it end up, up side down on a quite ordinary Victorian building in Chesterfield? Sir Richard's motto, 'Extremos pudente redisse', (ashamed to return last) casts no clue and the case of the busy bees of South Street remains a mystery, unless you know better!

Sir Richard Westacott's statue of Mary, Queen of Scots, at Hardwick is just one of many works in Derbyshire, but there is still no explanation why his coat of arms (below) should appear in South Street, Chesterfield

Suffer the Little Children

The early years of Chesterfield's Poor Law institute

T HE LITTLE GIRL, trudging along Newbold Lane in heavy boots a size too large, holding tightly to the hand of a lad not much bigger than herself, may have gazed up in wonder at the houses of the merchant princes, newly built in Abercrombie Street and screened by iron gates across the road. The orphans would have been in the crocodile that three times each week was taken on its airing from the forbiddingly gaunt building overseen by the mighty and good Board of Guardians.

These Guardians were spawned by the Poor Law Amendment Act of 1834 and took over the responsibilities of the Vestry and the annually nominated overseer for the poor throughout the parish. And the Poor? They were unchanging. Those who through old age, infirmity, disability, disease, unemployment or the misfortune of birth were unable to look after themselves made up this piteous group at the bottom of the very hierarchical social scale. More than half of them were children either orphaned or in families so large that they could no longer be supported or were simply unwanted.

The numbers in this deprived group had risen alarmingly from the end of the Napoleonic wars and Parliament became increasingly concerned at the growing cost of welfare relief. The way it was paid as out-door relief had led to a downward spiral in agricultural wages and a demoralisation of the poorest labourers. A Royal Commission led to the recommendation permitting parishes to unite and pool their resources to build new union institutions to provide relief in exchange for in-door work.

Chesterfield already had a commodious workhouse, built in 1725 close to the town bowling green, which according to Ford was well managed and housed about 30 inmates in 1832, whilst five times as many drew out-door relief. It rose to over 120 six years later and peaked at nearly 300 temporarily while the Bakewell and Ashover new buildings were completed. Ford records that the comfort of the unfortunate inmates was a major concern of the managers at all times.

But the town fathers were beguiled by the prospect of greater efficiency and economy in costs and negotiated with neighbouring parishes to put up a new, much larger building which would be shared by the poor of most of the western parishes of the Hundred of Scarsdale and be managed by a board drawn from each subscribing parish.

The 37 Guardians were drawn from the ranks of the merchants and traders, all justices automatically being members. Three were nominated in Chesterfield and there was a feeling the Chesterfield interests might be swamped, but they seem to have upheld their interests well, possibly because the vice-chairmen were J.Ps. both from Chesterfield. Amongst the first of Chesterfield guardians were Thomas Wilcockson, William Robinson and John Mugliston, who resigned after only six months because of the demands of the post.

Although the existing workhouse was too big for Chesterfield alone it was too small for the joint parishes so a new building was commissioned. A suitable site on Newbold Lane was soon identified and the land purchased at the end of 1837 from Joseph Gratton. It lay on the opposite side of the road from Holy Trinity Church still under construction at a cost of £3,300 and where the sixth Duke of Devonshire had laid the foundation stone earlier in the year.

The Guardians were anxious to produce a good utilitarian design which would combine efficiency with a pleasant exterior that would not be prison-like and while reassuring the inmates would

old almshouses on Newbold Road, Chesterfield

male inmates of the workhouse

hold out no inducement to the idle and profligate to enter within its walls. They visited Mansfield, Belper and Derby City seeking ideas and produced a brief for the architects Scott and Moffatt. The design in red local bricks was softened by some stone work. But its projected cost was too high. The Guardians debated long before agreeing to cut out the stone embellishments and the special wing, designed for the mentally impaired, to reduce costs. The contract was soon let for £9,000 (a third more than originally authorised by the London Poor Law Commissioners), and although it led to the bankruptcy of the builders it was completed on time, the first residents moving in just before Christmas 1839.

From the start the new building was too big for the prospective clientele and for the first ten years it was grossly under used. It housed all of Chesterfield's poor deserving relief including a number classed as imbeciles and lunatics, a special cell being provided for the care of the latter. More than half the inmates were children.

Finding staff with ability and sense of vocation was difficult. The first matron's appointment was a disaster leading to early dismissal for "improperly conveying provisions" out of the workhouse.

A part-time medical officer was appointed as was a school teacher. The curriculum was severely restricted to ensure the children would learn what would be useful in getting their living by the sweat of their brows. It concentrated much on instructing the boys on how to clean knives and forks, shoes and windows though some were lucky enough to be taught the rudiments of shoemaking in the work-shed. Teachers had a low status in the 1840s; the schoolmaster, who worked full time, being paid £5 less than the part-time Chaplain who read prayers and preached a sermon in the Union chapel each Sunday and administered the sacraments quarterly.

The food was very basic, men getting a third larger ration than women and children much less. But it kept body and soul together and was probably better than that served to many outside the rather forbidding walls. The in-mates were not prisoners. They could be discharged by their relatives or to take up employment but if they left and then could not support themselves they were punished severely.

211

Many of those on relief in the 1830s were the stocking knitters who at the turn of the century had been the highest wage earners in the town and had suffered from the change in fashions and the law restricting French imports. It was their children who could no longer be supported at home who found their way through the mud on their outings along Newbold Lane and wondered what life was like in Hurst House, Abercrombie Street, the home of the draper Francis Hurst, the Chairman of the Board of Guardians.

The Death of Coal

W HEN MICHAEL HESELTINE announced the final annihilation of the deep mined coal industry in 1992 he sounded the trumpet that brought an end to a very long tradition. In less than a year there were no operational deep mines left in north Derbyshire.

Coal mining in the county dates back to Roman times when outcropping coal was easily extracted. By the Elizabethan and Stuart periods there were coal pits at Eckington, Tupton and Chesterfield. Celia Fiennes recording in 1697 on her visit to Chesterfield that 'the coal pits and quarries of stone are all about even just at the town end'.

All the pits were small being limited by the size of the market they could serve. The product was bulky and of low value so that transport to a customer in Brampton, even from a mine in Hasland, more than doubled the pit-head price. The improvements made to roads with turnpiking made little difference and, though the Stockwith canal helped open markets to the Chesterfield collieries, it was not until the railway age that the industry boomed and pits able to supply the burgeoning London market opened up to the east of Chesterfield.

These new collieries were much deeper than those close to the town for the profile of the coalfield shows the middle and lower coal measures turning upwards and outcropping at Chatsworth; they again outcrop and, deepening as they run eastwards to Chesterfield, they again outcrop just below the surface of Shelton Gardens. This bump towards the surface continues towards Brimington before starting to plunge steadily deeper as they run towards the North Sea as the 'concealed coalfield'. Much of the coalfield is fractured and faulted so that seams are displaced upwards or downwards relative to their neighbours, a feature that made planning of collieries difficult. But, over time, a knowledge of where faulting might be expected improved the commercial viability of what was always a

fairly hazardous undertaking.

Some seams were so thin that they were not workable and so were unnamed. But, by the 1920s,despite eighty years of fairly intensive working, fourteen seams were still being worked in north Derbyshire where the thickness was around one-and-half metres. This was a world away from the two-foot seams in the Brampton pits of the 1840s where boys under 13 years old made up to sixty journeys a shift dragging, on their hands and knees, a woven hazel corfe containing just over 55 kilos of coal. Such work was frequently performed by girls and women in Lancashire but at least no females were employed underground in Derbyshire.

The worked seams were often named to reflect their thickness or physical properties at the pit where they were first worked - but occasionally with more romantic names for reasons that are now lost in the mists of time, The seams run without break into the Yorkshire coalfield where the seams' names will be different from those in Derbyshire. In Derbyshire there were the Clowne, Hazel, Top Hard, Dunsil, First and Second Waterloo, Bottom Ell, Deep Soft, Deep Hard, Piper, Tupton, Threequarter, Yard and the deepest, Blackshale. Even within this area there were naming differences, part of the Hazel being called Main Bright (considered a colourful name for domestic user coal) and some of the Deep Soft being called The Chavery.

The chemical make-up of these coals, and hence the purpose for which they were most suitable, varied but not as much as the coals of the South Wales coalfield. The coals in that field covered the whole spectrum from hard anthracite, which contains virtually no volatile content so that it burnt almost smokelessly, through to the high heat-content coals with little ash that won them Admiralty contracts in the hey-day of steam-driven battleships, on to the smokier house coals and the softer coals suited to making coke or for the gas works.

In the early days of mining around Chesterfield the hard coals found a ready market with the potters of Brampton and the lime burners of the Peak, while the softer croyzable coals, especially those fairly free of arsenic, which melted when heated and fused into coke, were snapped up by the brewers to dry malt. The Top Hard and other hard coals that fused when heated in an oven, particularly if their phosphorus content was minimal, made hard coke prized by the iron smelters. Over time these coals were worked out and the remaining Derbyshire coking coals had to be blended with the output from other coalfields to make lower grade coke more suitable to the needs of bakers and the domestic boiler. When Glapwell pit was sunk in the 1880s by the Sheepbridge company some of its coal was found to be cannel coal (which burnt with a long candle-like flame) and was found highly suitable for gas making and found a ready market in Leeds and Birmingham- but even this market was closed with the discovery of North Sea gas. The domestic market captured from the Durham sea-coals by Stephenson's Clay Cross company, via the London and Birmingham railway, was a major consumer up to the creation of smokeless zones when more and more of north Derbyshire's output was taken on merry-go-round trains running continuously to the power stations by the river Trent - with only small seasonal trains carrying small packets of fuel to the sugar-beet manufacturers of Norfolk.

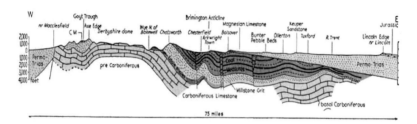

It was this flexibility of the coals to match available markets that kept the coalfield's economy buoyant.   During the early 1870s companies were finding money to sink new pits at an incredible rate so that inevitably there was overproduction when boom times would be overtaken by depression; in the late 1870s collieries were reduced to working only three days a week, with the workforce being driven to near penury through no fault of their own. But in retrospect these periods of low output were few and optimism soon returned to the Bolsover Company, for example, which sank   the Bolsover and Creswell shafts in the 1890s immediately following a depression that had closed down Boythorpe colliery. Similarly after the First World War, with all its upheavals, the Staveley Company, anticipating a decline in the iron and steel markets, decided to concentrate on coal mining and invest heavily in its Markham pits.

Over the century-and-half of intensive working many north Derbyshire pits were exhausted, but many had the potential to go on working for another ten or twenty years   until Michael Heseltine struck. Today as you leave the motorway at Junction 29   you see no sign to Glapwell or Ramcroft collieries and as you travel past the wooded hill, once Willamthorpe pit tip which screens you from the old Holmewood collieries, you little think that as you pass along the by-pass   into Chesterfield   you literally will go over the Bond's Main pit shaft.

It's fortunate that there are memorial pit wheels erected at Grassmoor, Clay Cross and Poolsbrook   to remind us of our mining past.

ACKNOWLEDGEMENTS

In preparing these pieces I have drawn heavily on the published work of too many authors to list individually. I acknowledge my debt to them and to the staff of the Local Studies section of Chesterfield Library and the Derbyshire Record Office at Matlock who have been very generous in giving me all the help I needed. *David Jenkins*